MISSING PIECES...

BROKEN HEART

Becca,   1-17-2018

   I know you will enjoy reading this book, especially when you read your street story about "Jaz". It is touching and inspiring to everyone who reads it.

   Thank you for sharing your story and allowing me to include it in my book.

   I hope our paths touch one day. Continued success in all you do and the good you do for so many...

     ♡ B. J. Shonk

Missing Pieces...
Broken Heart

A Recovery Guide for the Grief
and Sorrow of Pet Loss

B.J. Shonk

MISSING PIECES...BROKEN HEART

A Recovery Guide for the Grief and Sorrow of Pet Loss

ISBN   978-1-61961-740-7   *Paperback*

   978-1-61961-741-4   *Ebook*

This book is dedicated to all the amazing pet owners who inhabit our earth.
Those millions upon millions of devoted two-legged human creatures who
have shared their hearts as they developed deep endearing relationships
with incredible animal creatures of all persuasions. Our animal family
become our precious pets and caring companions, and we love them all.

To lose them is devastating beyond words.
Whether your special friend left too soon,
or you were blessed with many years of companionship together.
Whether you were crushed by their unexpected disappearance
and feel the pang of heart-wrenching uncertainty.
Perhaps your companion is sadly beginning to show the imminent, irreversible,
and unstoppable natural signs of aging and their quality of life is diminishing.
Possibly your pet is plagued and distressed by disease,
or painful disability has overtaken their body and their time is drawing to its close.
Or it was simply your pet's time to leave this life.
LOSS is LOSS...whether their death has already occurred, or is imminent and impending.
It all hurts beyond comprehension or expectation.
Time is a priceless treasure,
and we could never have enough of it with them as part of our lives.
When we know we will be losing a pet, our heart begins to break.
When we actually lose our special friend,
our hearts are painfully consumed and continue to shatter beyond measure.

I am also dedicating this book to my significant other—
my devoted friend, the love of my life
and special two-legged best buddy—my husband Randy, who shared the devastating loss
of our puppy girl Wookie. We took the painful journey together. He has inspired, assisted,
and encouraged me to pen this book as a healing tool and resource to help others.

My deepest desire is to provide pet owners with compassionate and useful information
to help mend your broken heart as you embrace
and celebrate the joy of your pet's precious memories.
I dedicate this book to each and every one of you.

Contents

Foreword

BY JESSICA QUILLIVAN, DVM

I met Barbara and her family on a fateful day in October 2015. I remember it like it was yesterday. She came with her son, Will, to see me in a time of crisis. Their miniature schnauzer Wookie, over sixteen years old, had been having seizures.

At that moment, I felt two very different emotions. First was the dreadful sorrow that, at her age, Wookie's time was very limited. I was already beginning to grieve for her family. Second, I needed to stay calm to be able to discuss, clearly and slowly, what Wookie's medical options were, and how we should proceed. I needed to be a veterinarian with clinical knowledge and skill, but I also needed to be a friend who could share emotions, experiences, and guidance in this time of extreme stress.

As a veterinarian with almost twenty years' experience, I'm often faced with situations like this. Veterinarians and veterinary staff commonly experience "compassion fatigue"— what the American Veterinary Medical Association (AVMA) describes as "secondary traumatic stress"—because they empathetically take on the burden of ill or dying patients with whom they have a unique relationship.

We get into the profession out of loving and caring for animals, but we often also see the terrible things that can happen to them, such as abuse and neglect. Then there is the emotional drain of losing patients—whether they are pets we've known their entire lives or ones we have just met. I think it's important to acknowledge veterinary team members for the endless work, time, and love we commit to every animal and human we serve.

I'm not sure if it's easier to lose a beloved animal friend suddenly, from an accident or acute disorder, or after a long course of treatment for a chronic ailment. Regardless of how it happens, it is always a very traumatic time for everyone involved.

I know this feeling well, because I am also a pet owner who

loves and cherishes each animal who comes into my life. At first, there seems to be nothing that can fill the emptiness in our hearts when a beloved pet dies. Some people feel guilt. Others feel anger. All of us feel deeply saddened.

I have always loved animals and knew as early as my elementary school days that I would one day pursue a career in veterinary medicine. I own and work in two animal hospitals. I have both a day practice, focused on general veterinary care, and an emergency practice. The biggest difference between the two is the degree of trust and bonding that develops with the families of the pets I treat.

In a day practice, there is often time, sometimes many years, to build a relationship with the patient and family—a relationship that can be very helpful when facing a decision about *quality of life*. Often, in emergency practice, no such relationship has been built. I'm frequently seeing the patient for the first time, and the family may be in crisis, seeking skill and guidance for their beloved pet.

I encourage all family members, whether you have known your veterinarian for ten minutes or fifteen years, to have an open dialogue about your pet. Do this, if possible, during every office visit and at all stages of your pet's life. Discuss problems and ask questions about general care, diet, exercise, or behavioral change. The more conversations you have, and the more active the role you take in your pet's health, the better the veterinarian can serve both you and your pet.

The veterinary oath includes a promise to "prevent and relieve animal suffering." I feel this is one of the most important aspects of my job. Making the decision to euthanize a faithful companion is likely one of the hardest we may have to make in our lifetimes. I consider it my most important mission to help pet families make this decision when necessary. I hope to relieve some of the suffering and pain that comes with such a decision by sharing my knowledge, compassion, and experience.

I never want a pet owner to feel guilty about making this decision, or to feel weak because of how sad they are after the loss of a pet. While such sorrow is becoming more accepted, many people feel ashamed or embarrassed that they are grieving so deeply for their pet—sometimes more deeply than they grieve the loss of family members.

I want everyone to know that grieving for the loss of a pet is normal, and I believe this book will help spread this vital message. It is important to talk about your loss and share your feelings, while continuing your normal daily activities. It is also important to realize others in the family may be grieving, and to reassure them they are still going to be cared for.

This includes other pets. Animals really do feed off our feelings, which is why we love them so much. It is important for their healing to continue their normal routines, and even add extra play and family time. This helps us heal, too!

Introduction

Every time I look at the gorgeous Venezuelan vase displayed in the art niche in my hallway, I think of the day Wookie accidentally broke it.

My sweet, spunky schnauzer loved nothing more than to chase a tennis ball through the house. My then-teenage son, John, was indulging the Wookster with a round of her favorite pastime when our overzealous pup crashed into the vase and sent it shattering to the floor. Anticipating my displeasure, my poor son raced to the cupboard, grabbed the glue, and got to work putting the broken pieces back together.

My beautiful vase looked awful. None of the pieces fit correctly, and glue was seeping out of the cracks. It was a mess. I knew it would never be the same again. As I looked at the damage, I cringed, but couldn't help but laugh. John was sincerely sorry, and I told him not to worry. He was quick to tell me he had "fixed" the vase. What can I say? Things happen.

A sweet Venezuelan friend of mine named Onexie, who fortunately happens to be a very skilled artist, graciously agreed to take on the task of damage reconstruction by filling and repainting the inside and touching up the outside and seams, all of which was quite an undertaking. She worked her magic, and these efforts improved on the extensive damage significantly. It was still obvious the vase had been broken and repaired, but I wanted to keep it regardless. I still wanted to display it in our home. It was a beautiful art piece originally; now it evokes precious memories. It is priceless!

Years later, after our darling Wookie passed away, I learned about the ancient Japanese philosophy and art of *kintsugi* and realized why that vase remained so important to me. *Kintsugi* is rooted in the idea that when pottery is broken, you mend it but do not try to disguise or hide the damage. You use platinum, silver, or gold to make a special glue to bind the broken pieces. This accentuates the breaks and makes them beautiful. The art piece becomes more special and endearing because it has a unique history and was treated with love. It is priceless because of the memories attached to it.

My vase holds a precious piece of Wookie's life. I'll never see it as broken, but as a beautiful, cherished vessel mended with my friend's tender warmth and skill. It holds the memory of Wookie playing with John that day, filled with life and joy that will live on long after her death.

We can do for our hearts what *kintsugi* does for pottery. When we experience the loss of someone we love, we cannot disguise the heartbreak. We can, however, mend our hearts in a way that celebrates the beauty of the love we felt for them.

Every person who has ever owned a pet has dealt or will deal with the loss of an animal. I have taken the journey several times and found the grief exceptionally devastating. It's been one of the worst things I've ever had to experience in my life. Like many other pet owners, I found myself particularly susceptible to the profound impact of losing my beloved friend and companion.

Even when we know loss is inevitable, it can be devastating. When Wookie reached age fifteen, I began to think realistically about the fact that we wouldn't have her forever, and our time with her would one day soon be coming to end. She was still spry, but she did sleep more and occasionally needed shots for mobility. I could tell she was getting older, even if I did not want to acknowledge this to myself.

Wookie was always tiny, weighing just around twelve pounds, and I started making it a point every day to pick her up, hold her under my chin, nuzzle her, and say, "Time to hug a puppy." I did it intentionally, with the understanding she could go any time. I wanted to create a sweet memory I could cherish about the last days with her. I am so glad I made the time to hold Wook and cuddle her close to my heart. I did it so much, my son Will started to do it too! I will never forget the first time he walked in the door, put her under his chin, then sweetly smiled at me, and said, "Time to hug a puppy." He knew; he understood; he got it.

We have to appreciate pets and understand we will not have them forever. Death is a companion to life. Everyone is going to live, just as everyone is going to die. When we acknowledge and take responsibility for how we react to that, we become empowered to positively press forward when the fateful day arrives. And it will come for all pet owners, often unexpectedly. We also must understand that the grieving process takes a long time. Unfortunately, today we are used to quick fixes in our society, but certain things in life require a process. This is a process that takes time, knowledge, understanding, and lots of patience.

WHO ARE PET OWNERS?

Pet owners are people who fully welcome an animal into their hearts and homes. When I refer to "pet owners," I am acknowledging those people who engage completely to develop deep, lasting relationships with their animals. We nurture them completely, care for their well-being, and love them unconditionally. Not all pet owners are positively and actively engaged with their animal companions. Some pet owners neglect or mistreat their animals, just as some parents neglect or abuse their children. These are not the people I'm talking about when I talk about "pet owners."

When you're a true and dedicated pet owner, the pet is much more than merely property "owned." To some, the word "owner" might even seem a little brash relative to the bond we develop with our pets. That connection is deep and very real. Our pets become an integral part of the family and our lives. You serve them. You sacrifice for them. You care for their well-being. You fully engage in adopting this special animal, whether big or small, into your life, and, in return, they give so much back.

On the other hand, there are some people who currently

own or have owned animals, yet somehow just don't develop that special relationship. There are also people who perhaps have never owned animals, and don't necessarily understand the development of this deep attachment and bond to family pets.

Pet owners who invest in the relationship forge a partnership of love with their animals. These companions become ingrained in our daily routines and habits; we even make sure they're included in our family photos. They truly become part of the family unit and are precious to us.

I'll never forget the first time I took Wookie to the vet and they called her back for her exam by asking for "Wookie Shonk." It hit me, in that moment, that she was truly and "officially" a member of our family. Even her name reflected it.

In many cases, pet owners love and care for their animals
just as they would a child. Some couples become pet owners
together before they have children. This was the case with
my son Chris and his bride Myrna with my grand-puppy
Leia. Some people spend more time with their pets than
they do with any other living being. My grandparents
Samuel and Sylvia raised Pomeranians, and as a young child
I can remember my mother Marjorie on occasion feeling
a bit frustrated. She would say sometimes it appeared my
grandfather loved his dogs more than his grandchildren.
It wasn't that he didn't love us, which he did of course, but
he only saw us a few times a year. He lived with his dogs

every single day of his life, along with his wife, and they were his family. He was a true pet owner who loved and cherished his furry companions.

As I fondly reminisce, I see my grandfather, whose nickname was "Red," and my memories flow. I remember this same man, who was a big fellow in stature and size, transforming completely in an instant when he interacted, played with, cuddled, or petted his dogs. He was huge, and they were tiny. I actually liked that simple sweetness about him, his love and the timeless bond he shared with his pooches. Our pets have the amazing ability to bring out the best in us. We may be flawed, but they don't see us that way.

Single people of all ages, empty nesters, and older couples often have pets who are their only live-in companions. They sleep with them, eat with them, take walks together, watch movies with them, take them hunting, fishing, or on vacations, and even talk to them. Of course, these activities are not solely for single or older pet owners—they are applicable to pet owners across the board, in all categories and age groups. We do so many things with our pets. They cannot get enough of us!

I used to talk to Wookie every day. She did so much with our entire family, and we have a pretty big crew. She took turns sleeping with everyone and snuggled up close in our beds. We never knew who would be her special bed buddy, as she chose different companions nightly. She loved sharing our popcorn, one of her all-time favorite treats, while cuddling close for family movie nights. She walked with us for miles on end to help us get our daily exercise. The Wook learned quickly that it was extremely advantageous to sit close to our infant grandkids when they ate in their high chairs. Plenty of crumbs made their way to her down on the floor.

There is a deep, unconditional love between pet owners and their pets. These beloved friends don't care what you look like, how old or young you are, what you're wearing, or even if you showered that day. When you have a pet, you have somebody in your life who totally adores you and truly believes you can do no wrong. You are their absolute hero, and isn't it nice to be someone's hero?

In some cases, pet owners are able to handpick the pets they want to become part of their family from a kennel or shelter. Some welcome animals into their homes who have been rescued or abandoned by their previous owners. These pets often come with a history of misuse or neglect, and that creates a different bond altogether.

Sometimes, pets come into our lives in ways we could never anticipate. I know of a woman named Becca who was working as a vet tech in Pittsburgh. It was Palm Sunday, and one of her clients was coming in to pick up his hospitalized dog. He brought with him a days-old puppy he had found abandoned in the parking lot. The staff put the small animal in an oxygen chamber. He wasn't moving and didn't even register a temperature. They prepared to euthanize. But when they came back to the tank, the pup was alert and nosing around. He clearly had a will to live. His tiny body was so small and in grave danger, but Becca and the rest of the staff nursed him back to health, and he survived. Feeling such compassion for this tiny guy, Becca decided to adopt him as her own, and he lived a long and happy life with her and her family. She named him Lazarus, in honor of his triumphant return from the brink of death.

When we got Wookie, I likened it to adoption, another subject very near and dear to my heart as the grandmother of several adopted grandchildren. On occasion, a few people have asked if I feel differently about my adoptive grandchildren than I do about my others. I always say, "No, they were just special delivery." Similarly, pets come to us in many unique ways. No matter how they come, we open our hearts and welcome them into our home.

Being a pet owner comes with great responsibility. You can no longer dash out the door at a moment's notice. You might even find yourself having to make sacrifices that are often inconvenient, just as you would when raising a child. My husband and I have missed a few big family gatherings because we had to stay home with Wookie during an acute illness. You change your plans, just as you would if your child was ill.

Pet owners also often bear the immense responsibility of caring for their pets at the end of their lives. They must act as their advocates and make difficult decisions on their behalf. Some of these are extremely heart-wrenching, difficult *"Quality of Life," or QOL,* decisions.

QOL

Quality of Life, referred to throughout the rest of this book as *QOL*, is the pet's overall well-being, the ability to live comfortably and happily, and do the things it loves to do free of pain and suffering.

MY SEARCH FOR HELP

In October 2015, my family and I lost our beloved dog Wookie. The circumstances of her death were devastating, and the pain that followed was unbearable for us all.

I'd lost various pets throughout my life, but Wookie's death affected me in a way unlike any other. She'd been with our family for over sixteen years and was very integrated as a precious part of our lives. We all shared a deeply developed relationship with her: our children, grandchildren, and friends alike. When we had to make the painful decision to have her euthanized, the devastation was excruciating. None of us were equipped to handle her *EOL, or "End of Life,"* that fateful day we never want to, but know in our hearts will come.

EOL

End of Life, referred to as *EOL* throughout the rest of this book, is the state of the pet's life as it approaches death. Pet owners often must make tough decisions during this time regarding the pet's health and well-being.

I didn't fully understand all the feelings I was experiencing. They were all so new and painful to me that I began desperately searching for help and understanding. I scoured the Internet for hours, reading reviews, trying to find the book I so wanted to work for me. I wanted something that combined both a personal and professional approach, including a veterinarian's wisdom about coping with the loss of a pet, coupled with the insight of pet owners who understood and could relate from their own personal experiences. As I listen to others who have shared the same experience, I have learned so much. Knowledge is a powerful tool.

The information I was finding often felt fragmented and, at times, confusing, rather like a puzzle with missing pieces. My search left me feeling overwhelmed and confused. From the books available, it quickly became obvious there is a very definite need for valuable and insightful information for pet owners who will soon be experiencing the loss of an elderly or illness-stricken pet, those contemplating euthanizing their companion, or those who have just gone through this painful loss.

You feel loss even when it is just a possibility. You feel it when it is impending, and you certainly feel it when it has recently occurred. I sincerely appreciate the fact that other people have penned and shared their experiences, but I knew I wanted something a bit different to help me navigate my own situation with a unique personal and professional edge. I felt exhausted trying to find that particular book. It would have helped me significantly if my vet had given me such a book during this time of profound pain and need.

Finding necessary medical information and advice about loss in a prompt and efficient manner during time of need is vitally important. I can relate it to another life-changing experience my husband Randy and I shared in spring of 2015, several months before we lost Wookie. He was diagnosed with cancer. Let me share his words:

As my wife and I managed the journey of my cancer discovery—surgery first, then a few years of follow up—the doctors always provided us with educational and enlightening written information to help us understand what was going on, what to expect next, and how the road to recovery looked. This information was extremely helpful and so beneficial when provided directly by the attending medical staff. This act of "informational compassion" allowed us to develop a much closer relationship with the medical staff while we were traveling a difficult road we had never before traveled or understood.

To our surprise, when we experienced the loss of our family pet Wookie, we found a real lack of written information immediately accessible to help us through the process ahead and to our emotional recovery. When we compared the lack of written information during our pet loss experience to what I had received in my personal medical journey, it became crystal clear we could do better at helping by providing others taking this same path of emotional recovery from pet loss with valuable information. This information could be easily obtainable through veterinary medical staff or purchased individually.

That is the purpose of this book: to help the client, to empower the veterinary medical and support staff, and to help build better relationships between a veterinarian and their clients.

Many of the books I found dealt only with death, but pet loss can be about much more than the animal dying. The pet owner will experience an entirely different set of emotions depending on how he or she loses the pet, whether it goes missing, is lost, dies during a surgical procedure, or runs away. Some people must find new homes for their pets because of their own declining health, aging, physical disability, or changes in family circumstances. Some lose pets because of divorce or a move. Some people experience *anticipatory grief* when they know they'll have to have their pet euthanized within a few hours or days. Some people experience sudden and shocking loss if the animal is killed in an accident or lost in a natural disaster. I wanted a book covering all aspects of loss. A loss is a loss, plain and simple. It all hurts.

ANTICIPATORY GRIEF

Anticipatory grief is the sense of deep sadness and despair we feel when we know our pets will not be with us much longer. They have not yet passed, but they are in the process of dying, and you begin to prepare yourself emotionally and mentally for the loss.

No matter how you have lost a pet, you will suddenly find yourself having to make hard practical decisions. How will you tell your children? If the pet has died, how will you handle their remains? How will you stay focused to do the things you need to do and maintain a normal routine? These questions only scratch the surface of the many things you will need to consider as you traverse the journey of pet loss.

You also must deal with the softer, more emotional aspects of loss. What do you do when you come home and see their toys? There is no sweet purr or warm swish of fur that caresses and curls sweetly around your legs when you enter the room. No one is waiting anxiously by the door awaiting your arrival and return. What about when you are ready to take a walk and your walking buddy is no longer there? How do you adjust to the absence of the jingle of their collar, which you've become so accustomed to? Where is your cuddle buddy and furry companion? No sweet serenade of song from your feathered friend fills the air. Perhaps you want to take a ride on your horse companion, and they are not there anymore. The soft side of loss can be heartbreaking. It is a heavy blow that hits the heart hard and hurts immediately.

Grief is like a journey, and oftentimes you don't have a map to help you understand where you're going. Because of my husband's career in the oil industry, I have traveled extensively domestically and overseas and lived in many places, including Texas, California, Nigeria, Kazakhstan, and Venezuela. Every time we embarked on a new journey, I did extensive research beforehand to make sure I understood as much as possible about the new location, area, country, and culture. I came to each new place as prepared as possible. Yet, there was always a series of unforeseen factors to be discovered along the way. Grieving without an understanding of what you can expect is like traveling to a foreign country having done no prior research. You wouldn't know the language, the culture, or what to expect. You wouldn't know how to get help. You would be lost. Being educated and prepared makes all the difference in the world in adapting and adjusting to changes in life, especially the difficult ones.

You cannot heal to the best of your ability unless you understand the journey. You must be willing to put in the time, follow a few guidelines, and reach your desired destination—a place of peace. The goal and objective are to mend your broken heart.

A DIFFERENT KIND OF BOOK

I decided to write this book so that no one has to look as hard as I did to find help at a time when they need it most. Quick access to valuable information is imperative, as we learned through our medical journey with Randy's cancer. It was a real eye-opener when the information we sought when we lost Wookie was not close at hand. There was a complete lack of something unique partnering the wisdom, knowledge, and personal experience of both veterinary professionals and pet owners who have walked in your shoes. We learned that compassionate and educational information at a time of need is so important.

It became clear in my mind again that, had my veterinarian been able to give me such a book on dealing with loss, it would've made a significant difference in my recovery process. Knowing the book had her stamp of approval, I could've immediately gained some understanding of what was happening, which would have been an invaluable gift.

Establishing a relationship with your vet based on honest, open communication can help during your pet's life and is especially important when facing tough decisions related to EOL. Their guidance can prove invaluable and is especially important at a time of loss. They deal with this devastation daily. This book can act as a powerful tool for veterinary professionals to offer pet owners who are grieving or anticipating the loss of their companions.

This book is for anyone who has ever lost a pet in any way, whether through death or any other circumstance. It's for pet owners, pet companions, children, families, and friends of pet owners who want to learn more to offer their love and support at this most difficult time.

It's also for those dedicated caring people working at animal shelter and rescue facilities, foster caregivers, and the veterinary staff who work with pet loss on a regular basis and experience *compassion fatigue.*

COMPASSION FATIGUE

Compassion fatigue is often experienced by caregivers as well as people who work in the medical and veterinary professions. It is extreme stress and, at times, trauma, caused by frequent exposure to the suffering of others.

This book will help guide you through the grief process and help piece your broken heart back together by covering such topics as:

🐕 Understanding that pet loss comes in many different ways and circumstances. Each type of loss is unique unto itself.
🐕 Dealing with and understanding grief, which presents itself in many ways depending on the unique circumstances of your loss or impending loss.
🐕 Developing a meaningful relationship with and draw-

ing upon the expertise, guidance, and advice of your veterinary professional and their caregiving staff.

- Better relating to and understanding compassion fatigue, QOL, and EOL as they directly relate to your pet, veterinary staff, and losing a pet.
- Dealing with the practical issues related to the death or loss of a pet, and the impending anticipatory loss of a pet who may need to be euthanized.
- Recovering from grief and taking personal responsibility for your recovery.
- Learning the steps to take and ways to positively progress on this difficult journey.
- Putting compassion in action to work in your life by reaching out and helping others deal with the loss of a pet, including friends, family, veterinary staff, and animal caregivers in all capacities.
- Recognizing how the loss can affect children and other pets in the home.
- Understanding when and whether it is appropriate to get another pet.
- Mending your broken heart from pet loss and positively moving forward to find joy in your life.

The piece of your heart you gave to your pet might never fully heal, and your life might not feel exactly the same as when they were with you, but you can learn to mend and find the peace you so desire. You'll learn to understand how your pet changed you and made you better. You can turn the pain of missing them into an appreciation for the time you had, just as I have done with the memory of my dear Wookie. Our life shared with our beloved pets is a gift to be cherished, appreciated, and savored, even when they leave us. Memories are indeed etched in our hearts forever.

Wookie the Schnauzer

OUR PUPPY GIRL, OUR FLUFFY COMPANION

The best and most beautiful things in the world cannot be seen or even touched. They must be felt with the heart.

—HELEN KELLER

My life has led me on wonderful adventures, many including my sweet Wookie. Before I tell you about her, I'd like to tell you a little about me.

MY BACKGROUND

I live in the Houston area with my retired husband, Randy.

Our family has long had a connection to the area and Texas in general, though life has taken us many different places. Randy's work in the oil industry required frequent moves, which included a decade living overseas in Nigeria, Kazakhstan, and Venezuela, and the opportunity to live on the West Coast in the San Francisco area.

In West Texas, I worked for the *Odessa American* newspaper as a journalist and as the Newspapers in Education manager. I promoted literacy through a partnership with the Ector County School District, local businesses, and various broadcast media outlets.

I also have a business background, having owned my own company in Houston for over eleven years. American Modeling Incorporated focused on self-improvement programs for women and girls and fitness-awareness programs for children.

A common thread throughout my life has been the desire to help mentor people of all ages. One of my favorite experiences was teaching teenage orphans how to speak English in Kazakhstan. In return, they taught me Russian and Kazakh. It was very sweet to see such young people wanting to emulate those they looked up to. Although I served as their mentor and teacher, in reality I was the one most being taught and learning valuable lessons about life, similar to the way pet owners are taught unconditional love and so much more from their cherished pet companions.

I've also learned a great deal from my large, wonderful family. Randy was my high school sweetheart, and we have been married more than forty-five years. We have eight amazing children, twelve grandchildren, with another on the way, four grand-puppies, and a grand-kitty. Each child is special and endearing, just like each pet we own throughout our lives. Having such a large family is a unique experience by today's standards, and it has shaped me in ways I could never have imagined. Being actively engaged as a pet owner changes your life profoundly as well.

I've had pets my entire life. Most recently, I was a pet owner to Wookie. We had just gotten her when we learned Randy's job required a move to Venezuela. She came along for the adventure, and we lived there for over five years. During our other two assignments overseas, it was highly recommended we not take pets, and we had to make special arrangements for Wookie. Family members, including Randy's sister Nancy, took turns living in our home back in the states and cared for Wookie in our absence. Wookie even became the official dorm dog at Texas A&M, where our son Aaron was studying. We missed her just like we did our children, grandchildren, and friends during these overseas assignments. When we called home, it was always so wonderful to hear her barking in the background and sending us her precious pooch greetings from afar. It warmed my heart to hear our sweet Wookster.

We did whatever we needed to do to make sure she was well cared for and happy, which is simply what pet owners should do. Our puppy girl, as we called her, was literally part of the family. That bond, as any pet owner knows, is what makes the loss so difficult.

I experienced several different pet losses as a child, but Wookie was my first as the pet owner. We had her the longest, and she became important to every person in my life.

The loss of Wookie, coupled with my background in helping people and our journey with Randy's cancer, is what motivated me to write this book for pet owners, veterinary professionals, their staffs, and animal caregivers of all kinds. There are ways to overcome the challenges you are facing and see your situation in a new light. I've been there. I know the pain of a broken heart from pet loss. I also know if you are actively engaged and take upon yourself the personal responsibility for your recovery, you can overcome your grief to progress positively forward.

MY PET LOSS EXPERIENCES

Each of my pet loss experiences happened due to different circumstances and resulted in different forms of grief.

CHARLIE

When I was four years old, my family got a fabulous white spitz called Charlie. I didn't have any brothers or sisters yet, so Charlie was everything to me. My mom was pregnant at the time, and I couldn't wait to have a sibling as well. Life was good—or so I thought.

Then unexpectedly one day, Charlie was gone, I could not find him anywhere. I asked my parents where he was and they simply said, "Charlie doesn't live with us anymore." I couldn't believe it. I asked every question I could think to ask. *Did he get sick? Did he die? Is something wrong? Can I see him again?* They would only tell me they were afraid Charlie might not like the new baby, so he had a new home. *Whose home? He belonged with us!*

I was devastated and confused. Suddenly, I felt a bit strange about getting a sibling, because it meant my dog had to go away. I never understood how my family could get rid of our dog without talking to me about it or even giving Charlie a chance to acclimate to the new baby. I think my parents were trying to do the best they could. They did what they did out of love and concern, and just didn't know what to say or how to explain the situation to me, but it still hurt.

GIGI

After losing Charlie, I asked my parents for another dog regularly for years. Finally, when I was around ten, they brought home Gigi, a sweet little tan miniature poodle. I adored her. I have wonderful memories of playing with her and snuggling close together. I had a brother and sister by then, and Gigi got along great with everyone. She had a gentle and caring nature, and enjoyed playing with all the neighborhood kids.

One summer day, we were playing out in the backyard, as we usually did, when Gigi started convulsing and fell over. I didn't know what was wrong or what to do. Gigi was only two years old. I remember thinking to myself, *this cannot be happening*. I was afraid to hold her and I didn't have time to go get help. She had a seizure and died right in front of me!

It was my first experience with death of any kind. Although I was young at the time, I have never forgotten that sad day.

BOOTS

After the traumatizing loss of Gigi, I didn't have a pet again until I was in junior high. My mother had remarried by then, and my stepfather wanted us to have dogs. Boots was a cute black-and-white mutt. She loved to sit on our laps and was extremely sweet-natured and very loving.

Unfortunately, my parents did not keep Boots fenced in, and she was allowed to wander freely throughout the neighborhood. Everybody on our street got used to seeing her walking around, gave her treats, and loved her, but I still always worried about Boots getting hurt. We lived on dead-end road, but there were busy streets nearby, and I knew an accident could happen.

One day, I was walking home from the bus stop after school when I saw Boots lying on the side of the road. She had been hit by a car. It was terrible. I knew she had been killed because she was not properly cared for, having been allowed free range to roam. To this day, I do not understand why such an avoidable death had to happen, and it still hurts. I loved my Booter. I felt cheated again. She was not yet two years old. Losing pets at an early age is indeed a harsh reality for many pet owners.

RUSTY

At the same time we had Boots, we also had a beautiful Irish Setter named Rusty. After Boots was killed, I paid much closer attention to Rusty when she was outside, as it would have been devastating to lose another dog so tragically. After a few years, my father decided he didn't want to have dogs anymore, and we needed to find Rusty a new home. I decided I would try to oversee securing a new home for her.

Randy, who was my boyfriend at the time, also loved Rusty. His mom and dad were dog lovers and Rusty's friends. With that already in my favor, I decided to ask Randy's parents if they would like to take Rusty. Eileen and Larry were willing and kind enough to adopt her into their home, which meant I could still see her! I was elated that Rusty was going to be part of Randy's family, and I could continue to see and spend time with her. I remember she loved to follow Eileen everywhere around the house, lie down by Larry's side when he was working in his woodshop, and just have fun running around their safe, fenced-in yard. She was very happy in her new home. Rusty was well cared for and lived a nice, long life with her new pet owners. She was always so excited when I came to their home and overjoyed to see me. I was so happy she could remain accessible to me and that I could continue to have her as a special part in my life.

CASEY

I did not have another pet until years later, when my children were young. They desperately wanted a dog, and my parents, Marge and Tom, kindly offered to get them one for Christmas. We picked out a tan cocker spaniel who somewhat reminded me of my darling Gigi from my own childhood, and the kids named her Casey.

But Casey was nothing like Gigi. She was small and tan-colored, and that is where the similarity ended. Her temperament and personality were completely different: she had an aggressive nature.

Our family tried to develop that special relationship with her, but she never truly fully bonded with us. Unfortunately, she did not feel like a real part of the family. She had a mean streak and just did not bond with or embrace our family, especially the kids, the way we had hoped, despite being loved and well cared for by everyone.

One day, Casey nipped at a neighbor boy. It didn't break the skin, but it still sent up a red flag in my mind. Soon after, she bit one of my sons close to his eye. This behavior was not acceptable and was dangerous.

Randy and I had a difficult decision to make. We knew we had to step in and advocate now on behalf of our children.

We knew we couldn't have a dog who was not family-friendly, nor could we, in good conscience, give her away to another family because of her sporadically negative temperament. We called the Humane Society, explained the situation, and they were able to take her. We hoped she could receive the special help she needed. I remember the white animal truck from the Society and the man who took her away. Again, I cried.

Everyone, including my mom, felt bad, but we were not comfortable having Casey in our home. It broke our hearts to have to let her go, but we knew it was for the best for our family. Sometimes, hard choices have to be made.

Shortly thereafter, the kids were yearning for another animal. I was a bit leery, of course. There was a cute, sweet-natured stray cat that frequented our yard, and the kids asked if they could start feeding and play with her if she stayed outside. I met the cat and she seemed sweet, so I allowed it. "Missy Kitty" kept coming back to the yard. The kids enjoyed her—and so did I. I was actually preparing to take her to be examined by the vet to make sure it was okay for her to play with the kids. I also wanted to learn more about caring for a cat. Unfortunately, shortly thereafter, her wandering nature caught up with her, and she was hit by a car. The kids spotted her along the busy roadside just over our fence. It was another sad day for us. As a result, our family needed a break, and we went without any kind of pet for years, until a certain schnauzer captured our hearts.

Aaron as a teenager with his "Puppy Girl" and best fuzzy pal—Wookie.

WOOKIE

We were living in West Texas in the late 1990s when our youngest son, Aaron, started asking for a dog. He was around ten years old and approached me very matter-of-factly. Randy and I liked to take walks—mostly to preserve our own sanity in a house full of children—and Aaron had come up to me before one of our strolls. He said, "Mom, I really want a dog. We haven't had a pet in a long time, and I know Casey didn't work out, but I really want a pet. Would you do me a favor? When you go on a walk with Dad, would you please talk him into letting me have a dog?"

I told him I would give it a shot. I told him no promises, but I would try.

On our walk, I told Randy about the conversation. He laughed and smiled sweetly. He totally understood, having had and loved dogs all throughout his childhood. He agreed it was time to welcome another dog into our family. Mission accomplished on my part, and Aaron's dream came true. He was one elated little guy!

As a family of allergy sufferers, we wanted to stick with breeds that wouldn't irritate our symptoms. I researched various breeds, and this time we agreed on welcoming a miniature schnauzer into our crew.

We paged through the want ads and finally found a family with a litter of miniature schnauzers right in our own town. Aaron and I went to visit them. There was a litter of five: two females and three males. We decided we wanted a female, and Wookie was simply too cute to pass up. As the runt of the litter, her brothers towered over her. She fit in the palm of our hands. She also shared something special with Randy: a birthday. It was meant to be.

We couldn't bring her home right away, as she wasn't weaned off her mother's milk. We had to wait a few weeks, and during that time I traveled to Austin to be with my oldest daughter, Melanie, who was preparing to have her second child, our first granddaughter, Brooke. A few weeks after the birth, I returned home, and there was Wookie. Randy had taken the boys to pick her up, and I was overjoyed. I had just left a new baby girl in Austin and was welcomed home to a new fluffy baby puppy girl! Life was good.

When we put her out in the backyard, she was still very tiny and she toppled over the blades of grass. She was just this adorable little silver-and-white fur ball. We could not help but love her. I still had three rambunctious boys living at home who all loved *Star Wars*. I think they owned every *Star Wars* toy on the market. We decided to have a special family night devoted to naming the dog. Their first choice was Chewbacca, Chewie for short. I didn't love it. I suggested

Molly. They unanimously gave me the big thumbs down. We all thought some more, and the perfect compromise presented itself. I didn't want Chewie, but Chewbacca in fact was a Wookie. We had our name.

Sweet times of Sarah and Wookie sharing good times simply playing in the grass.

From the start, this sweet, fun animal changed everything in the house. She quickly became the light of our lives. The kids loved her, as did all their friends. She was a total tomboy. She simply fit in and could keep up with the crazy pace of her boys any day.

Everything was going great for a few months when, lo and behold, we found out we would be relocating overseas. "Excited" was not the word—another family adventure was just around the corner. We knew we wanted to take Wookie with us, and that meant she had to go through all the preparation we went through, including medical exams, inoculations, official documentation, and special notarized affidavits. What a tedious project! It is a significant amount of work taking your pet family member overseas. During the chaos of preparing to move, Randy wondered out loud if we would have ever gotten Wookie had we known what the future held with our upcoming international move. The boys were totally incensed. "Don't even think about it, Dad," they said. "Where we go, the dog goes." That was it—conversation over.

Wookie came and lived with us for five-and-a-half years in Venezuela. It was wonderful. We walked her everywhere around the Caribbean marinas in our apartment complex. The neighbor kids fell in love with her. She became the unofficial mascot for the international school the boys attended. Each afternoon during the week, she would wait patiently and sit staring at the door for them to return home after school. She chased tennis balls all over the apartment. As we strolled around the marinas along the coast, she would gawk incessantly at the sea gulls that flew overhead and watch the waves crash against the shore. She constantly tried to run after the huge resident iguanas, always hoping to catch one. On each occasion, I tightly held the leash and was not going to let her dream come true. Despite not capturing iguanas or other native creatures, she was constantly happy and totally in her element.

John, Aaron and Will with their Wookster. She adored her boys!

During this time, we also had the opportunity to have our son, Doug, live with us for a summer before he went back to college. The Wook now had four energetic buddies who spent lots of time with her. He used to take his three younger brothers out in the bay wakeboarding, snorkeling, and exploring islands. Of course, Wookie loved to tag along with her boys to supervise all the action and excitement. She wholeheartedly embraced the wind blowing on her face on boat rides with them, and loved strolling the sandy beaches when we all went island hopping and exploring as a family together.

After we moved to California, Wookie and I would walk

Randy to work every day. Then, just the two of us would head to the park, where we would spend hours walking and playing. There were scores of wild turkeys that often gathered around the playground in our Central Park, and she loved to try and catch them. Her attempts luckily always failed, again with me holding her leash close in hand. We could even walk to her new vet's office, which was conveniently right across from the park. Wookie was always comfortable there and loved Dr. Sandy Block and her wonderful staff. Relationships are forged and developed one visit at a time.

Strolling through the redwoods in Central Park was a daily adventure during Wookie's time in California.

Aaron lived with us for a short period, while he worked and saved money for college. This, of course, made the Wookster very happy, especially at night when she snuggled and snoozed next to him. There were also many times Randy traveled for work, and then it was just Wookie and me. She was my walking partner, movie buddy, cuddle partner, and little shadow. My sweet fuzzy pal.

Wookie lived to be sixteen-and-a-half years old, a nice, long life. However, just like any other dog, she endured her fair share of dicey situations.

CLOSE CALLS

While we were living in Houston, Wookie fell ill on the Fourth of July. We were supposed to go to a special family get-together, but Randy and I stayed home to tend to her. It turned out she had suffered a tick bite and had to be rushed to the emergency clinic for treatment. The vets told us a full blood transfusion might be necessary. Randy and I had to decide whether that was something we were we willing to do. We weren't sure we wanted her to have to go through that. Thankfully, it wasn't necessary: the prescribed medicines worked, and Wookie pulled through.

Once again in Texas, we nearly lost her when she crawled through a tiny hole under our fence, unbeknownst to us, and ended up in a neighbor's yard. Shortly thereafter, I could not find her and began panicking, remembering her previous fence-escape incident. I assumed she had gotten out just as before. I called and called for her outside and looked everywhere. Finally, I went inside, looking around the entire house, and headed into my son's room upstairs. Lo and behold, she was totally chilled out, buried under his mound of covers, sound asleep. What a relief! She had simply been sacking out with Aaron, and he had left for school. I laughed and was so grateful that I found her safe. A new memory and fun family story had been created.

Another incident occurred when Randy and I were living in Nigeria, and Wookie was staying with Aaron, who was now attending Texas A&M. She fell critically ill with an intestinal virus. Fortunately, the College Station area is one of the best in the country for veterinary care because of the university, and he was able to get her the quality care she needed. They ran many tests, she underwent treatment, and again she survived.

Later, we were living near San Francisco when Wookie was around ten years old, and while petting her one day, I felt a lump near her throat. It was cancer. Our vet, whom we had a great relationship with, was concerned about the location of the lump, as removing it could affect her ability to bark or eat. Dr. Sandy Block wouldn't know how impactful extracting it would be until she was able to get close to it. We went ahead with the surgery, and Wookie survived with no complications. She flourished and lived another six-and-a-half years. This is a great example of the importance of developing a good working relationship and partnership with your vet. Not being afraid to ask important questions, communicating as a team, and being your pet's advocate, whether it is a routine examine, a possible surgical procedure, QOL, or EOL situation, are vitally essential.

I could fill an entire book with stories about Wookie, just as any pet owner could about their own family pets. Your special stories are precious, too. It will be important to document them to share with those you love. They will always hold a special spot in your heart. These cherished memories are part of the reason losing a pet hurts so deeply. Wookie changed our lives and made me a better person, which is why, in the end, I knew I had to give her "the last gift of love" and let her go with grace and dignity. I'm sure there are many wonderful ways your own pet changed you forever.

LOSING WOOKIE

In fall 2015, Randy and I traveled to Colorado to see Aaron and his wife Taylor. Another son, Will, was living with us at the time, while he studied for his master's degree, and was happy to care for Wookie whenever we were away. It was a responsibility he took very seriously. He took wonderful care of his fuzzy pal. If he was unavailable to tend to Wookie while we were gone, we would board her at our veterinary clinic, Shady Brook Animal Hospital. I developed a good relationship with and had complete confidence in her primary care veterinarian, Dr. Jose Salazar, along with the professional staff at the clinic. We appreciated Wookie's wonderful boarding tech, Brittany—especially her informative daily email updates and fun photos!

Will took Wookie everywhere. She'd sit on his lap while he studied, sleep in the same room right beside him, and was his attentive car-washing assistant. He often called Wookie one of his best friends. When he was studying, his full-time assistant was the dog. Where Will went, the Wookster was sure to follow.

We were traveling home from our trip when Will called.

"Mom and Dad," he said, panic in his voice, "Wookie had a seizure. She's groggy and incognizant and doesn't really know what's going on. It didn't last too long, and I think she seems to be coming out of it. I know you're going to be home tomorrow, but I just wanted to let you know and give you a heads up." He explained he had to work an evening shift at his job at a nearby grocery store, but his twin brother John and his wife Emily would be coming to care for Wookie and spend the night with her.

The rest of the trip home was pure agony. It would be hard for me to describe the anguish and pain it brought into my heart. I could not stop thinking about my sweet girl and what was happening to her. We stayed in close contact with the family, and John reported that Wookie had suffered another seizure on their watch. This was my first experience with the heartbreak of anticipatory grief. Randy and I knew in our hearts the prognosis for two seizures within a matter of hours for our sixteen-year-old puppy girl was certainly not good. Every minute of the long drive home that day was heartbreaking. We left the hotel early that morning, October 31, Halloween Day.

When we finally made it to our driveway on Saturday afternoon, we saw Will outside with Wookie near his legs on the grass. She was teetering, toddling, and walking incoherently. She looked at me and had absolutely no idea who I was. I knew instantly something was seriously wrong.

I lunged out of the car, grabbed her, and held her close. We called the vet, but they were dealing with another serious emergency and suggested we take Wookie to their sister clinic, an after-hours, weekend, and holiday emergency-care facility, which we had never been to previously, but was owned by the same doctor.

We called and they told us to come right away. Randy stayed home and Will came with me so he could explain to the vet all that had transpired. Before we made it down the driveway, Wookie went into a third seizure. In one of the most heart-wrenching moments of my entire life, I watched as she foamed at the mouth and convulsed profusely while I held her on my lap. Will told me this seizure was the worst one yet. My grief awareness was rising.

We made it to the clinic and the staff immediately administered medication to calm her down. We met Dr. Jessica Quillivan, and she examined Wookie. She could not pinpoint what caused the seizures but told us the fact that three had occurred in less than twenty-four hours was a bad sign.

I panicked. "We can run tests," I said. "Money's not a concern. Let's find out what's going on, what's the path forward, what we can do, where is she at, how will she be?"

As I spoke, I took a step back and really listened to myself. I took a deep breath. I needed the care, concern, and expert advice of our attending vet. I needed to slow down, focus, and listen, so I could properly evaluate this difficult situation.

"Doc," I said. "Just be honest with me. If Wookie was your dog, what would you do?"

"First of all, Mrs. Shonk, we can run tests for you," she said. "We can do anything you want to do. But, I must tell you, the dog you will be getting back is not the dog you have had."

She paused.

"If this were my dog, I would put her to rest," she said. "I would let her go."

I heard her words and steadied my heart. I decided in that moment that if Wookie had another seizure, we would euthanize her. I cared too much to see her failing so quickly right before my eyes. Her QOL and comfort were everything to me. I mentally prepared myself for the next step, the EOL, and Dr. Quillivan told me it was okay to take her home and observe her. That way, Will and I could talk with Randy about the seriousness of Wookie's terminal condition and Dr. Quillivan's recommendation.

The instant I walked out the door with Wookie in my arms to head home, the fourth severe seizure hit. It was time. No more. Decision made. It was time. We walked right back through the door into the clinic. I handed her directly to the staff, and they gave her a shot to help relax and sedate her. Wookie never recognized either of us upon our return home from our trip.

I called Randy, and he immediately left to come be with us. In the twenty minutes it took for him to arrive, I thought about my decision. I knew in my heart it was right. Between Dr. Quillivan's words and the pain of watching my puppy girl suffer, I understood she could not go on. This was not QOL.

While waiting for Randy's arrival, Will and I took turns holding Wookie for the last time, and the tears flowed. I held her close, as my broken heart was anticipating what was shortly to come. There was no stopping it: the end was imminent. I made sure Will was able to have the most time with Wookie. He needed it. He was losing one of his best friends, and I was losing a sweet companion.

When Randy came into the room, he reacted just as I had initially. He wanted to know if tests were an option. "What about x-rays or an MRI?" he asked. "Money is no object."

I heard a familiar panic in his voice, as he echoed the exact sentiments from my conversation with the vet just a short while before. It was jarring to see my sweetheart and husband in such a state. But then I watched as he calmed himself, just as I had. He took a deep breath, held his hands in the air, and lowered them slowly to his side as he regained his composure.

"Whoa," he paused, took a deep breath, and looked Dr. Quillivan in the eye. "If Wookie were your pet, Doc," he asked, "what would you do?"

She reiterated that she would do whatever we wanted, but, in her opinion, the best choice was euthanasia. Randy looked at Wookie, saw her totally sedated and resting, and agreed. We all knew what had to come next, even though none of us were mentally prepared for it.

Randy held Wookie and spent his last moments with her, just as Will and I had prior to his arrival, and we all cried even more. Dr. Quillivan explained that Wookie would not feel anything. The IV injection would simply make her heart stop beating. It would be quick and painless. She mentioned that occasionally there is a muscular reaction after the heart stops. It is not indicative of pain in the animal, but she wanted us to be prepared just in case it occurred.

She made the injection, and, peacefully, Wookie's sweet little heart stopped beating. We stood there together and let our Wookie go. We knew it had to be done, and we had made the right choice, but the pain was still unbearable.

"Take as much time as you need," Dr. Quillivan said, and we all took turns saying goodbye. We all gave our fluffy pup one last cuddle and kiss, and left. We returned home, utterly drained and completely miserable. I could not believe she was gone and had no idea what to expect next. None of us did.

LIVING WITH THE LOSS

When I walked into our home immediately after losing Wookie, I did not know what to do, how to feel, or where to turn next. I saw her dog kennel, her tennis ball, her bed, and her stuffed toys. Just looking at them made me feel as if I were drowning in fresh waves of grief. How can anyone possibly explain the pain and anguish? I was heartbroken that she never recognized me that afternoon on our return home from vacation, I wished so much she could have heard my parting words of how much I loved her and what she meant to me. Funny the things that immediately cross your mind at such traumatic times.

I put the kennel away. I hid her bowls, washed all her bedding, and packed it up. I gathered her food and unopened meds to give to our boarding tech, Brittany, so she could disperse them to other pet owners or keep whatever she could use for her own pet. Everything else got stashed out of sight.

I was a total mess. Randy was pretty teary-eyed, shaken, and quiet, but seemed to be doing fairly okay under the circumstances. There were, of course, the occasional teary-eyed and "losing it" moments for everyone, mostly me. But it wasn't until about a week later that Randy suddenly and unexpectedly really broke down, crying intensely. Wookie and Randy always shared a very special relationship. She was his little fluffy wrestling buddy. They would play hard, and he'd rough her up in that typical guy-ish play sort of way. Wook was definitely a little tomboy at heart, and with her boys all grown and gone, except for Will, she always looked forward to their evening playtime together. With the sweet, special relationship they had developed, all the pain, sorrow, anguish, and heartache surfaced in large measure that evening. He was missing his little buddy, too, and he just could not hold it in anymore.

"You miss her, too?" I remarked to Randy after he broke down.

"I do," he said.

"But you're doing so well."

"Honey," he said. "I'm doing so well because I have to. I have to be there for you. You need me to be strong."

It was so hard to see him in pain. Will grieved quietly by

isolating himself upstairs in his room. Within a few weeks, he moved to Colorado and stayed with Aaron and Taylor to finish his degree. He needed a change. This helped him press positively forward, so he could move on with his life. We let the rest of the family and our friends know about the loss, and the letters and calls poured in. They all understood our pain and felt the intense sadness, too.

As much as we tried to be there for one another, and as much as the support was appreciated, we were miserable. When you are grieving, there is nothing you can do but go through it. Everything changes, but you find ways to cope, some of which might surprise you.

Because we lost Wookie on Halloween, the holidays were right around the corner. Part of our Christmas tradition was dressing Wookie in this adorable elf costume. The grandkids totally loved it, and Wookie just went with the flow to keep everyone happy. It was not really her style, but, being a good sport, she did it anyway. When I found the costume, I decided to honor our cherished family member by putting it on one of the stuffed bears I collect. Hugging those bears also helped. I would close my eyes and cuddle them like I would Wookie, and the softness seemed soothing. Wookie was so soft and such a joy to caress, so hugging those teddy bears really made a difference at a time when softness warmed and soothed my aching heart.

I also found solace in a piece of artwork we have near our stairway. It's a picture depicting the Savior holding a lamb. I'd bought it for Randy because it made me think of him holding Wookie. The lamb was about her same size and had her same big floppy ears. One day shortly after losing Wookie, I glanced at the picture walking down the stairs, and in my mind, I heard the Savior say, "You know lambs hear my voice. Do you think for a moment my other creatures don't?" I knew in that moment He was holding

Wookie in His arms, and she did not want me to be sad. It was so powerful, and I've never forgotten that moment. It came to me when I needed it most. I am religiously oriented, and this incident is very powerful and real to me. But if you are not religiously inclined, no problem. Simply consider this a sweet touching story that soothed one broken heart.

Regardless of our religious beliefs, we all know that life and death go hand in hand. They're partners, companions. You don't get one without the other. We all live; we all die. We know we will lose people and pets along the way. Grieving becomes a part of life we must all accept, but knowing how to navigate it can make the journey less difficult.

THE GRIEF WAS EXPECTED, THE DEPTH OF IT WAS NOT

I always knew I would lose Wookie one day; I think all pet owners know in their hearts that our animal companions are a temporary gift. In most cases, pets rarely outlive their owners. My rational mind knew it was coming, especially toward the end of her long life. My heart, on the other hand, felt broken in places I didn't even know I had.

I went to church the day after losing her. I was physically exhausted, emotionally devastated, and drained. I didn't wear a bit of makeup, because I knew it would just end up running all over my face when I couldn't contain my tears.

A few people told me I didn't look very good. I explained we had just lost Wookie. Their response was typically the same: "Aw. I'm sorry." Then they'd walk away. A few people took a moment to embrace me. One person said, "You'll be okay. It's not like a family member. It's a dog." They didn't understand Wookie *was* part of my family.

Every time, I was left thinking, *You have no clue how I feel!*

I had to force myself to calm down and remind myself some people have never experienced the deep abiding attachment to a little creature like I felt for Wookie. I told myself not to let their comments upset me. *People don't say such things to inflict harm; they just don't understand.* My family loved Wookie, and she loved us back. Not everyone understands the pain accompanying such a loss. Unfortunately, not everyone has had the opportunity and privilege of establishing and developing an enduring pet owner and animal bond.

Later, while sitting in a meeting, I found myself feeling sad and depleted, when a friend named Christie sat down next to me. Without saying a word, she reached over and put her arm around me. I put my head on her shoulder, and I cried. It was exactly what I needed. She understood that for some people, the loss of a pet is just as devastating as the loss of a person. Pets are in your life all the time, showing you unconditional love and affection. The pain you feel in their absence can last, in some ways, forever.

The feeling of loss might diminish, but you will always miss your pet companion. You have to cry; you have to feel miserable. It is a necessary part of the grieving process. At the same time, you must continue to live. Life is about living and finding joy. Life does not halt because of loss. You have to get out and do your normal daily tasks. When you lose a pet, you don't lose everything else. That does not mean it is not difficult making the journey enduring the pain. You still have your family, friends, perhaps a spouse and children, your home, your job, and a life worth living.

To help navigate my own grief, I focused on my family, friends, faith, and the many other blessings I have. I also reminded myself often of how lucky I was to have had Wookie in my life.

Accepting the loss, however, does not mean everything is automatically tied up with a nice, neat little bow. You still must work through the grieving and loss process; there is no way to avoid it. If you don't allow yourself to feel it, you can become stuck and can't positively move on and press forward. Even if you accept it and find yourself feeling better, something unexpected will hit you and send you right back to the pain. A spot in your heart still needs to mend. It all takes time, and sometimes lots of it.

The sense of loss extended to everyone who knew us well. Our grandchildren would come to visit and observe that something felt off. "Your house doesn't feel the same, Grandma. We really miss Wookie," they would say. And it didn't. Wookie had been such a huge part of our lives, even our physical environment was altered by her death. The times when our older grandchildren came to visit or stay with us, Wookie was in total heaven, and so were the kids. Andrew, Brooke, Sarah, and Cash were all actively engaged buddies with the Wookster. She loved Phillip at first sight; they were instant pals. Losing her deeply impacted all our grandchildren, Eternity, Logan, Landon, and Leila included. She played with and developed special relationships with each of them. They were buddies. Our three youngest grandchildren did not quite have the same opportunity to make these memories.

There are very distinct chapters in each of our lives, with beginnings and ends. The sweet chapters with Wookie will be cherished and fondly remembered by our older grandchildren. Our younger grandchildren will have different memorable moments of their own to cherish and cling to.

I've found children to be particularly observant when it comes to coping with the loss of a pet. Our son Doug, his wife Melinda, and their kids raise chickens. They are like their pets: they care for them, name them, gather their eggs, and protect them. When I held my first chicken while visiting them, I was a bit surprised and taken aback at how fun they are to hold. The chickens were so soft and cuddly. I can understand why the kids become deeply attached to each of them. When one of the chickens, Georgia, died, our granddaughter Eternity was absolutely crushed. She was in so much pain, she wrote a poem about it.

Our Dead Pet

The chicken we love
The chicken died too young
So, all I did was grieve
She was a friend
All I did that day was grieve
It was a sad day.

Not long before that, Melinda's mom, Renon, had died. Eternity lost her other grandmother but was too young at the time to fully understand the impact of death and loss. But after losing Georgia, she went to her mother and said, "Mom, now I understand how you felt when Grandma died." She could relate to the grief her mother had suffered. It became real to her, as she had lost someone she loved and had cared and sacrificed for.

RECOVERY WITH A PURPOSE

No matter how we experience loss, it's painful. When I began my own grief journey, I desperately wanted a tool to help me along the way. However, extensive research proved unfruitful. I felt I had been thrown out on the ocean in a torrential storm and needed a lighthouse to guide me back to shore. I did not yet understand the journey one must take to find recovery with a purpose and attain inner peace. Finding information was crucial, and spending excessive time searching the Internet for it was not what I wanted and needed to do to ease my pain.

Recovery with a purpose is about learning from your painful experience and navigating positively forward. You must search deep within and ask yourself what you've gleaned from what you've gone through. What good has the pain done for you? For me, it was gaining the understanding that

Wookie was a precious gift. The gift might've only lasted a brief time, but in that time, she made a significant impact on our lives. Losing her was terrible, but her life with us had been a joy. Life is made up of many short chapters, and I was grateful for all of them I spent with Wookie. Our time together was worth every moment and memory we shared and created, especially now that she is gone.

The secret to attaining inner peace is appreciating what you have instead of dwelling on the negative. Many people go through hard times and never recover. They never press positively forward. They hold a grudge or ask, "Why me?" Other people realize life can be tough, but they use challenges as opportunities to grow and better themselves in ways they never could have imagined or anticipated. They take responsibility for how they react to the circumstances of their lives and succeed because of it. We cannot control all aspects of our lives or everything that happens to us, but we do have the ability to control how we react and how we press forward.

If you are empowered with useful information, remain positive, and use that knowledge, you can move past your grief. When traumatic things happen, you can either turn them around or let them destroy you. Avoiding grief when it's new can seem tempting, but doing so only sets you up for more pain and suffering in the long run. Face your loss and the reality of it, then press forward to recovery to find peace. Know that time, patience, sound information, and an attitude of gratitude are the keys to success.

The way you lose a pet, whether to illness, accident, disappearance, or any other circumstance, can significantly impact the way you grieve. Yet every heart is capable of mending, and there are tools to help you heal.

Loss Is Loss

LOSING YOUR PET TAKES MANY FORMS

There are some who think it's foolish to weep,
Over a cherished pet in eternal sleep,
But those poor souls are truly blind,
For they know not of the creature kind,
But you who devoted so many years,
Deserve the time to shed those tears,
Over the loss of your furry friend,
Whose life on earth has come to an end,
And may the tears that you now weep,
Sow loving memories forever to keep.

—UNKNOWN

When we think of loss, we generally think of negative things, especially pain and sorrow. We think of losing a loved one—often a two-legged family member such as a spouse, friend, parent, or even child. We think of losing a job or a home. Perhaps we think of losing mental or physical abilities, such as eyesight, physical mobility, or hearing loss, to disease or accident. We can lose money on investments or business partners. Loss can also involve positive change, such as when we lose weight or end a hurtful relationship, but in many, perhaps most, cases, we associate loss with pain.

At its foundation, loss means something is missing. Dictionary.com describes it as "the disadvantage or deprivation resulting from losing." Even in its simplest form, it is a powerful feeling. Think about how much momentary distress is caused by the simple act of losing house keys or your sunglasses. We can spend minutes or even hours of frustration trying to find what was lost.

The most powerful form of loss we can feel is the loss of someone close to us, whether two-legged or four-legged. This deprivation takes away from us in ways beyond our control. There is absolutely nothing we can do when we lose something we can never get back. We can, however, decide how we respond to the loss.

We all have control over how we handle pain. We can

control our reactions, negative or positive. As we face loss—especially pet loss—it is up to us to make the best decisions. It is both easy and tempting, sometimes unknowingly, to make poor choices in these situations. Pain makes some people want to lash out. Others want to push the pain away and not face or deal with it at all. None of these choices help us move past the pain.

We can, however, choose to react in positive ways. When we strive to make the best decisions possible, we commit to making positive changes within ourselves and then implementing those good choices. We choose to work through loss as it comes.

This is not easy, and everyone must do it in their own way, as each kind of loss brings with it a wide range of emotions. Yet the underlying grief is the same. I've personally experienced several different kinds of loss, and will pull on that knowledge to help guide you through your own grief. It is soothing to know someone understands and cares about your recovery.

HOW WE LOSE PETS

There are many ways and reasons we lose pets. All can cause us great pain as we work to understand and cope with our grief.

While our pets are with us, they fill our hearts and homes with joy. The feeling of happiness they provide us becomes something we almost take for granted. Then, when we lose them, their absence can leave a hole we didn't even realize was there.

DEATH

The most common form of pet loss involves death. Some pets go through prolonged illnesses or do not survive surgery. Some suffer unexpected accidents and are left with complex, life-altering wounds. Sometimes, our pets simply begin to age in the normal cycle of life itself, and we become aware of their physical decline and realize their death is approaching.

There have been many advances in health care for pets in recent years, but it is important to understand and realize such extended care is still typically short-term and QOL must always be our primary concern and objective. To prolong life for a pet companion who is declining and in failing health simply because it can be done is not always the best decision for the pet. When we truly love, sometimes we need to let them go in peace. In some cases, this means we have even longer to consider the impending loss, feel the ravages of anticipatory grief, and begin to ready our hearts for their EOL. Yet, even when we have time to prepare ourselves for the loss, the impact is not necessarily softened.

Death also can occur suddenly. My daughter, Stephanie, had two hamsters as pets when she was in junior high school. At the time, they were the only pets we had in the home, and she often let them out while she cleaned their cage or wanted to hold or play with them. She loved them completely, those teeny tiny pals. One day, her younger twin brothers, who were around five years old, saw the hamsters and decided they were very dirty and needed a soothing bath.

Thinking they were being helpful, they gave the hamsters that cleansing bath. They had no idea that this could hurt the animals. To them, it seemed a simple and straightforward way to help them get cleaned. To five-year-old boys, it made perfect sense that when something is dirty, you wash it to get it clean. They wanted to help their big sister care for her pets.

Entering her bedroom, Steph stumbled upon the scene and let out a scream the entire neighborhood could hear. The hamsters had not survived the bath. Her hamsters were gone, and at the hands of her brothers.

When they realized what they'd done, the boys were so very

sad. They also knew they were in trouble and hadn't meant to upset their sister. When I asked them what happened, they replied, "Mom, they were very, very dirty, and we were trying to help, and we gave them a bath. We weren't trying to hurt them. We liked them."

I pulled my daughter aside and talked with her about what had happened. We talked about her brothers and how they hadn't meant to hurt her or her hamsters. It was difficult for her, because she truly loved these tiny creatures. She fed them, cared for them, and sacrificed for them. One minute they were healthy and playful; the next minute they were gone forever. The pain of such a sudden loss was very real and ran deep.

DISAPPEARANCE

There is an element of uncertainty in every form of loss. We almost always begin our grief journey with the question, *What do I do now?* We don't know what to do next or what our lives will look like moving forward. Our hearts are heavy-laden with pain and grief. It just hurts so much.

This pain associated with uncertainty is elevated when we lose a companion to unclear circumstances. When a pet runs away, we face an overwhelming sense of the unknown. Questions arise that can't be answered: *What happened? Is she okay? Will she come back? Has someone taken her? Was she recovered and taken to a shelter rescue facility? Where should I start looking?* Until our pet is found, we lack closure. In instances when the pet is never found, that closure never completely comes. We face each and every day with the feeling that a piece of our heart is missing, and we feel helpless, unable to get that piece back. All we want to do is mend and feel relief.

A new resident in our development experienced this kind of loss soon after she and her husband moved into their home. We live in a wooded community, and, just a short time after they moved in, her dog ran away deep into the woods. What must she have been feeling about her new home? Instead of welcome and joy, she experienced loss and pain. Resolution and grief were intertwined for her, because her dog was never found. She asked herself terrible questions that had no answers. Was her pet eaten by a coyote or bit by a snake? Was it hit by a car? Was it trapped somewhere, unable to free itself from a fence or ditch? I am sure she agonized over such imagined scenarios, which gave her grief even more power over her. The uncertainty robbed her of a sense of closure.

Not knowing creates a terrible ache in our hearts—one that can't be calmed. We experience a change that is both physical and mental, and the pain alters us forever.

Around ten years ago, a large number of rural communities outside the northwest Houston Metro Area experienced the ravages and devastation of uncontrolled wildfires. They occurred while Randy and I were living in Kazakhstan, and we checked the Internet daily to learn about the extent of the damage near our property. The fires touched down in our development, not far from our property.

A sweet friend, Rose, and her family were not quite as lucky as we were. The wildfires reached her home, totally destroying it. As if that were not devastating enough, she lost several of her dear four-legged friends. As the fire engulfed their home and surrounding property, two sweet feline companions, her cats Simba and Mew, were lost, and two older family dogs, Roxy Raven and Bobbie, were as well.

Such fires are not uncommon, nor are other disasters such as flooding, tornados, or hurricanes, which unfortunately happen frequently in my home state of Texas. During these catastrophes, along with the destruction of personal property, many animals are lost or die every year. Natural disasters create their own unique kind of grief for pet owners. These animal losses, coupled with the loss of a home or other property, leave the owner with a great deal of complicated emotion to work through as they navigate their grief.

It has taken Rose a lot of time to positively move forward

from these horrific loses. Sadly enough, she is now also working through the recent loss of her Labrador, Kuro, who was hit by a car.

Loss of pets is indeed a cycle and continues to happen as long as we are pet owners. This is why is it so important to understand how we can take responsibility for mending our broken hearts. We will always carry sweet memories of the joy our pets brought us and the happy times we shared. They would not want us sad.

RELINQUISHING A PET

Sometimes, we lose pets because of factors related to our physical environments or changing life circumstances. Perhaps you have moved, and your new home is not conducive to pet ownership. Perhaps you've lost a pet to divorce or separation. Many things change in our lives: it is an evolution and progression every day.

I'm reminded of Casey, the dog we had to give up after she became aggressive toward the kids. Our children, though they were not to blame, went through feelings of pain and struggled to understand why she had to leave our family. That sorrow fell on my shoulders as well. I cared about her and even cried over the decision. But I had to hope that eventually a new home would be a better environment for her. For the safety of our family and our neighbors' children, it simply wasn't an option to keep her in ours. Perhaps her aggressive nature was never resolved; we never knew what happened or became of her once she was picked up from our home.

No matter the reason for relinquishing a pet, the grief is the same. A loss is a loss, and we must work through the pain to come to terms with it.

GUILT IN LOSS

Depending on the circumstances of the death, it is common for pet owners to experience a certain sense of guilt. Even when we are conscientious, things can still go wrong and leave us feeling responsible. Dogs slip off their leashes or run under fences. Cats sneak out the door and run away. They disobey commands, get loose, and endanger themselves. When these things happen, it is important to be compassionate to yourself and others. Bad things unfortunately do and will happen throughout our lives, but they are more than counterbalanced with the good and joyous pleasures and experiences in life. We always have to look for those with appreciation.

Another friend, Barbara, had gone out for a little while, and her husband had stayed home. Her dog Luke was in the backyard, playing on a leash, when it wiggled loose and squeezed away. Without her husband Allen realizing it, the dog had gotten out, run into the street, and was hit by a truck. My friend came home and found her dog gone and her husband in complete agony. It was time for compassion to rule and love to lead the way. Instead of reacting in anger, she realized the importance of her role in helping her husband heal. She thought, "I can't have him feel bad. He in no way wanted that to happen. It was an accident."

She consoled her husband, hugged him through his tears, and told him she loved him and that he shouldn't feel bad. He couldn't have known that was going to happen, and he wouldn't have meant for their dog to get hurt. We sometimes have to let go of our anger and pain to console and extend extra love to those who love us. Kindness and compassion are perfect partners in healing.

Barbara could have reacted negatively and become angry with her husband, blaming him for what happened. This is often the easiest response. But she made the positive choice to react with love and compassion. Though this was the more difficult choice, she made the decision to support him and, in the process, helped her own heart to soften, heal, and mend.

While he likely was reliving the scenario again and again

in his own mind, her husband also had to find a way to forgive himself. We must remember accidents do happen. Often, there is no rhyme nor reason to them, and assigning blame is useless.

When those feelings of guilt become rooted within you, you must find a way to show yourself compassion. Not every accident can be prevented. You can't fix or avoid every mishap. You're human. We are all human and fallible. You need to be able to say to yourself, "I wasn't trying to do anything wrong. That was not my intention. I feel terrible, but I have to get over this. I have to get past it." Mistakes, tragedy, and unfortunate accidents are all part of life. Don't let guilt rob you of your joy and happiness.

LOSS IS LOSS

No matter how it happens or how long we have our pets, whether it is two months, two years, or twenty years, losing them still means we've lost. We simply hurt. The pain is still real, and we grieve for them. Regardless of how long a pet companion has been in your life, the emotional bond has already been formed. While the loss may feel different, it still has a huge effect on who we are, the choices we make, and the things we do from that point on.

The loss of a young pet can feel just as devastating as the

loss of a pet we've had for many years. There is no minimum age or time requirement for loving a pet. The bond and attachment are real and profound. It happens quickly and is cemented deeply within us when we bring a sweet companion into our home and our family, and welcome them into our heart.

ANTICIPATORY GRIEF

One of hardest parts of being a pet owner is the knowledge that, in most cases, we are going to outlive our pets. It is the ultimate reality and truth. We might be able to put those thoughts aside for some time and pretend our pets are going to be around forever, but once it becomes clear that death is approaching, we have no choice but to face this harsh reality. No pet or person lives forever. There is a time and season for all of us.

Once again, it is vitally important to fully acknowledge and understand the deep impact of anticipatory grief, that heart-wrenching sense of deep sadness and despair we feel when we know our pets will not be with us much longer. They have not yet passed, but they are in the process of dying. They might be sick or severely injured. You might have made the painful decision to euthanize, and you look toward the next phase with dread and fear, as the EOL approaches. This kind of grief can be just as intense as the grief we feel for pets who have died or been lost, if not more so in some cases.

I experienced an intense, albeit brief, feeling of anticipatory grief when I lost Wookie. Knowing she was having seizures, we found the ride home from our vacation excruciating. She was experiencing seizures we couldn't stop or control, and they were taking her away from us a little at a time. I knew as we drove home that we probably would have to let her go. Had we run tests or been able to treat her condition temporarily with medication, it would not have changed the ultimate outcome. She might have ended up losing mobility or existing only in a vegetative state. The grief I felt in anticipation of her loss could have swayed me to pursue such options, but, in the end, I would have only felt worse, believing I should have made the choice to give her that last gift of love with dignity.

Losing loved ones is always hard, and making the best choices for them in those challenging times can be just as difficult, especially when the decision is euthanasia. Even after you have made the painful decision, you have to say goodbye. In some cases, this might happen very shortly after the decision is made. In others, you have the opportunity to take your pet home temporarily and spend a few last hours or days with him or her. That time is precious, since you know that with every passing second, your time with your pet grows shorter. You can't get it back, and it will come to an end more quickly than you imagine. It won't feel real.

Since I experienced grief myself, I have taken time to talk with others who have also lived through this scenario. Almost unanimously, they say they were grateful for the last bit of time they spent together, but also felt completely miserable because of the anticipation. The grief was over-whelming before the event even happened!

This makes me reflect on my special buddy Patty and her sweet Buffy. Patty and I have been friends over fifty years— talk about a human bond and deep friendship—so her story is especially close to my heart. Buffy ironically came into her life as a result of a very persistent request from her sister, Linda, who was then the foster animal caregiver for this tiny little Labrador puppy. Patty was a bit apprehensive, as she and her husband Don had lost a precious pet, Misty, whom they had owned for over ten years, and their home environment had now changed significantly. They were not quite in "getting a new pet" mode and phase when Linda persistently began making her request to Patty. Their two sons, Brad and Brian, were grown and off to college, and Patty and Don were now basically empty nesters.

This would be a huge lifestyle change. They would have the deep responsibility of becoming devoted pet owners all over again. Linda insisted that "this yellow ball of fur was perfect and meant for them." Patty knew it was time to talk to Don, and assumed his immediate response would be no. But to her surprise, he said "yes." Linda was elated she had won, and the couple immediately began a new journey and adventure with a four-legged family member.

Buffy changed their lives and shared nearly sixteen wonderful years with them as their buddy, confidant, resident fluff-ball, cuddling pal, and traveling companion. Because the boys came home frequently during their school breaks after their parents initially brought the new puppy home, all three of them became quickly acquainted and instant best buddies. Patty said that Buff would, "go crazy when her boys came to visit, never wanting them to leave."

This privileged pooch enjoyed traveling and living in dual residences. She spent summers up north and, during the cold winters, became an official furry snowbird residing with her owners in their winter home in Florida. Here was a Lab who loved life! She was in pure heaven, laying her head on Patty and Don's shoulders when they traveled down south or to stay with the kids.

Unfortunately, as it does with us all, time brought the new and unwanted changes of advancing age, degeneration, and declining health. Buffy's eating habits and other issues started to surface. Her vet discovered a tumor on her spleen. Because of her advanced age, the vet vetoed surgery. At this point, Patty and Don had to simply watch and wait, love her, and take good care of her. There was to be absolutely no jumping, rambunctious playing, or wrestling matches with Don anymore. If Buffy did too much physically, she could rupture her tumor and bleed to death.

Patty and Don realized their days and time with their sweet companion were coming to a swift closure. Shortly thereafter, Buffy was barely eating or drinking water, and had some vomiting incidents. Another vet visit determined the tumor was growing rapidly. The doctor recommended euthanasia that day. The dialogue quickly switched from QOL to EOL.

The pet owners decided that, rather than having the euthanasia done that day, they would take Buffy home for one last weekend together, and their vet agreed to do the procedure the following week. They were not mentally prepared to let go of their Buffy that day. They needed some time to digest, discuss, and prepare for the finality of it together. They had time on their side for those last few days together.

Unfortunately, in some cases like ours with Wookie, there is no time for a last weekend shared together, as euthanasia must be performed quickly in emergency circumstances.

This family weekend spent with Buffy was special, with memorable moments shared. Yet all the while, it also was one that carried the heavy weight of anticipatory grief, and all its associated pain and sorrow. They enjoyed their time together, and shared those last hours while Patty took lots of photos. The following Tuesday, she and Don gave their Buffy the last gift of love. The two of them sat sadly together on a blanket on the floor close beside their sweet Buffy and let her go in peace, as pieces of their heart shattered and broke beyond measure.

Anticipation adds a whole new layer to the grief process. Even if you know the choice you made is the right one, it can still rip your heart apart. You may feel pieces missing all over the place. In this instance, you must show yourself compassion and remind yourself that you are doing what you are doing because you care so deeply about your pet. You are willing to end their suffering, even if it hurts you. You put their QOL in the forefront and set aside your personal pain at not wanting to let your beloved pet go.

THE HOME

Another factor capable of affecting your grief is your home environment. When we got home after euthanizing Wookie, I looked around our home and saw everything that had belonged to her: her bowls, kennel, tennis ball, little mouse toy, bed, and other belongings. That first walk through the house was miserable. Everywhere I looked, I saw where Wookie once was. I knew she was gone and our lives had changed forever. It still was hard to comprehend and felt unreal. So much had happened within that painful twenty-four-hour period once her seizures began.

I knew being surrounded by all those reminders would only make me more miserable. I got a box, put everything that belonged to Wookie in it, and stored it away for the time being. It helped me acknowledge she was gone. It was actually a first baby step in the recovery process. You might find it tempting to take all your pet's items and immediately throw them away, because seeing them causes you too much pain. I encourage you to slow down, take a breath, and allow yourself time to grieve.

Letting go of your pet companion is a process that takes time, and there are healthy ways of dealing with the pain you're feeling. When you start looking at all those little toys and pieces from your pet's life, approach them with care. There's a difference between things you don't need, things you can give away, and little family memories and mementos. If you're not sure what you want to do, go get a little box to place things in until you can calmly determine how significant they are to you. There may indeed be some mementos you want to keep. Allow yourself that time to intelligently decide, and don't rush yourself. It's okay to step away and come back to this task. Be patient.

When I went back and began going through Wookie's things, it was actually very therapeutic. Suddenly and unexpectedly, I was able to start talking about the different memories connected with each item. Tears will fall, and you may get a bit choked up in the process. That is okay and normal. I was able to pick out some items to take to our boarding tech, Brittany, so they could perhaps be used for other animals. It took me out of my comfort zone, which affirmatively pushed me in a positive direction. Some people allow the pain of their loss to take over, causing them to feel like life has entirely lost its purpose and joy. Finding ways for others to use toys and items connected with your pet's life can turn your pain into something positive. Giving of yourself and sharing a piece of your heart are therapeutic. When we truly love, we give back to others. We become the beneficiaries. Joy slowly replaces pain, and the heart begins to mend.

GRIEVING AS A FAMILY

Just as your home will never quite be the same, neither will you or your family. If you have a spouse, children, and other loved ones, everyone feels a deep sense of loss, either directly or through you. Everyone must grieve and heal together, as well as individually. I know our older children, who had not lived in our home or perhaps spent only a short time residing with us when we had Wookie, experienced the loss as well. Chris, Melanie, Stephanie, and Lisa all loved her deeply, not to mention the four younger boys. She touched their lives as well, just as she did the lives of all the grandchildren, our children's spouses, and their friends.

Here is a touching note Doug sent us after we lost Wookie. It expresses sentiments of his heart through the foundational faith and principles we share as family:

Dear Dad, Mom, John, Will, and Aaron,

I was just thinking how all you have lost a true friend and member of our family. Wookie was a part of all our lives and we, the rest of the family, do love and will absolutely miss her. Especially the grandkids who could not stop talking about seeing her. She has seen our family through many blessed and happy times, some hard and difficult trials, but if there was ever an example of Christ in our family who never stopped giving love to everyone every living second she had in her 16 years. She is probably the best example of Christ's ability to love all no matter what. Maybe that's why Heavenly Father allowed us the opportunity to have specific animals as pets to show us his perfect ability to love. I know we will see her again as she is sealed to our family...just my opinion, but I know

I'm right on this. Our family sends our hearts and prayers to all of you right now.

Leila and I can't wait to see all of you this week. I LOVE ALL OF YOU SO MUCH!

Love extends beyond the miles and rebuilds broken hearts. There is strength in numbers when family supports family and friends reach out to one another. Married, single, young, or old, we are all people and want to reach out to one another, especially when the need is greatest.

If you are a parent, there will be times you need to put aside your own grief to make sure your children, regardless of their age, are okay. Reach out in full compassion, be honest with them about what has happened, and encourage them to talk about the memories. Consider well how you choose to approach the situation. It is important you help them understand loss is a part of life. This approach will be different with each child, depending on their age and maturity,

Putting your own emotions aside to help your children understand something so painful can be challenging.

Having others rallying around you can help. Whether it's your spouse, your friends, or your siblings, you need a support system that can help you step away from the trauma in your heart and mind, so you can progress individually and better communicate with your children.

I think back to the time we had to talk with our kids about Casey. We called everyone together for a family meeting. We all sat down together, and we said, "There's something serious going on. Tomorrow, some people will be coming by to take Casey to a new home." The kids were, understandably, initially upset, so we explained our decision. We told them that, based on her past behavior, we were concerned about somebody getting seriously hurt. We told them we loved Casey, but we had to do what was best for everyone's safety. The kids didn't like it, but they appreciated our honesty.

The conversation was not easy nor pleasant, but in the end, we knew it would help our kids better understand the situation and process loss. We later overheard one of our sons explaining Casey's absence to a friend. He told him Casey had to go away because she had bit some children, and she needed to go to a new home to keep them safe. The teachable moment had worked.

We will talk more about helping others, particularly children and other pets in the home, through their grief in chapter 8.

WHEN YOU LIVE ALONE

There's a difference in the way we love and care for our pets when we live alone. If you are single, you will also profoundly feel the impact of your loss. The devastation might possibly feel even more magnified and pronounced. It is an important time to seek out family, friends, and others you are close to. Find support in their love and comfort. Do not isolate your grief by thinking you must bear the painful burden of sorrow alone. A broken heart carries an immense burden and intensity that needs help and support from loved ones to counterbalance the heavy weight.

The pet companion becomes your only family in some ways. You spend a great deal of time alone together and rely on one another for companionship. This leads to the formation of a deep bond, a dynamic duo. Single people, widows, and widowers often form such relationships with their pets and experience a particular sense of loss when the animal is no longer around.

My daughter, Lisa, has a sweet cat named Lady Rambo. She knows all her unique habits and quirks, and can even tell when Lady is mad at her. It's obvious they need each other and rely on each other. Part of their routine is a nightly ritual when Lady snuggles up and sleeps on Lisa's pillow. Crazily enough, the cat tends to occupy and hoard most of the pillow. This is their routine; it is just what they do together. They care about each other completely. Now and then, my daughter will say, "Mom, I don't know what I'm going to do when Lady's gone. She's like my kid." Even the thought of one day losing her brings my daughter great pain.

SERVICE COMPANIONSHIP: SERVICE, GUIDE, EMOTIONAL SUPPORT, AND ASSISTANCE ANIMALS

For many, the role of pet owner means relying daily upon the unique services rendered by their trained animal companion. These animals are specifically trained to provide active service and offer support, guidance, and assistance to their human counterparts.

With a service-oriented companion, this specialized help, guidance, assistance, and support begins with the pet. An animal, often a dog, is brought into the life of someone who needs a trained companion for special assistance for a number of disabilities and needs, including vision problems, emotional support, or mobility needs. These animals help people of all ages. Horses can also act as service and emotional-support animals.

These specially trained animals act as companions and become an extension of the person they serve. This makes for a special bond beyond the normal pet owner and animal relationship.

Oftentimes, service animals are matched with veterans who are living with a disability such as Post Traumatic Stress Disorder (PTSD). They might be at a point of feeling there's no hope. Then the animal comes into their life and brings joy and assists them with their special needs. Their world is changed, and joy begins to fill their heart. That's unconditional love at its purest.

Because of the nature of the relationship, the owner of a service animal can experience a unique form of grief when the pet dies. They have lost both a loved one and someone they have come to depend upon physically or emotionally for service and companionship. When you know of someone who has lost their service animal, please take extra time to acknowledge their grief and be their friend in this dire time of need and loss.

PETS OF ALL KINDS: DEVELOPING, NURTURING, AND FOSTERING RELATIONSHIPS

As humans, we have the capacity to love all animals, from dogs to cats, chickens to goats, horses to hamsters, rabbits to reptiles, birds of all sorts, and every other possible pet on the planet. There is no limit to what pets we can love as our companions. Some have a stronger capacity for reciprocating that love, but nonetheless, the pain we feel when we lose them is real.

My buddy Miller loves raising and riding horses, and there was one who had become her close companion and best friend. One day, while transporting her horse Big Red, the trailer jostled and the animal seriously hurt its leg.

Because of the nature of the injury, they had to eventually euthanize Big Red. The loss devastated Miller. Her connection to Red extended far beyond the normal pet owner relationship. Miller had put her life in the horse's hands every time she rode him. The subsequent pain was so deep that her journey through the loss and healing process was significant and excruciatingly painful. She so desperately wanted to mend her broken heart and find peace. In time, she took responsibility and ownership of her grief, and pressed positively forward, as we all must. Red was only around three years old, which deeply accentuated the pain of loss. Miller felt cheated of the years of companionship she had anticipated they would share together.

Animals of all sizes can grab hold of our hearts. As a child, my husband, Randy, experienced such a bond with his pet parakeet. He would feed and care for the bird, and the bird would fly around serenading him and land on his shoulder. They enjoyed each other. But one morning, Randy awoke to find his bird lying on the bottom of the cage. He'd died in the night, and Randy still remembers the hurt he felt from the loss.

Children involved in 4H often raise everything from rabbits to pigs, cows, horses, and more. They begin working with the animals when they are just babies, care for them as they grow, then show them at the rodeo and local county, and state fairs. Though their animals are often sold, you can imagine the bond that forms when they raise these animals from such a young age. Hannah raised a goat for 4H and cherished the experience. She started caring for her goat and soon developed a deep friendship and connection with it. One day, her goat, Leonard, accidentally got out from the gate and was hit by a car. Hannah was devastated.

This brings up another special relationship somewhat similar in nature to that of young people who raise animals for 4H. Another type of "love and release" relationship is exemplified by those who temporarily provide foster care for animals in their homes. Those special people provide a temporary home for abandoned and rescue animals until a new adoptive pet owner welcomes them into their family.

My friend Patty's sister Linda often provided foster care to animals needing placement into a loving home. That is exactly how Buffy came into her life. Linda foster cared for her, and then Patty and Don adopted Buffy as a puppy into their home. It takes a special kind of a love and dedication to provide temporary foster care for animals in need, and attachments can form. It takes sacrifice to provide this kind of care, knowing you will one day be releasing that animal into the hands of a new adoptive owner. It is important we appreciate those people who provide this selfless temporary love to animals in need.

Foster pet care is especially important in times of crisis or natural disaster. We hope animals separated from their families can be safely returned, but that is not always possible. Caring for rescued animals in foster homes or shelter facilities is a vitally important component to helping them find new homes.

In the end, it doesn't matter whether an animal is covered in fur or feathers, scales or shells: a bond is a bond. The more you give of yourself to your pet companion, the stronger the bond. You sacrifice your time to be with them. But they also help us feel better when we are sick. When we are sad, they comfort us. You build unconditional love. Love is given and reciprocated from both sides. No matter the form that bond takes—whether it's pet owner and dog, cat, horse, bird, hamster, or fish—the devastation and heartache of losing your companion is real and deep.

Partnering with Your Vet

NOW AND IN THE FUTURE

Chance favors the prepared mind.
—LOUIS PASTEUR

Being a pet owner involves caring for animals in all aspects of their lives, especially their health. Just as you would seek out the most knowledgeable and caring pediatrician for your child, you must find a veterinarian with whom you can forge a solid partnership. That is exactly what we did with Randy's doctor and medical staff when we went through his cancer surgery. Good communication with any medical professional is vitally important in all scenarios and circumstances.

Establishing trust with your veterinarian is one of the most important things you can do as a pet owner. Not only will it help your pet stay healthy, it will help you understand all their needs, especially in times of illness or emergency and throughout your pet companion's natural aging process and mature years.

ASK THE TOUGH QUESTIONS

We started asking tough questions regarding Wookie's health several years ago, with the onset of her mobility issues. She was having trouble with stooping, bending, and balance. It was time to talk to our vet and set up an appointment to discuss my concerns. I was able to open up a dialogue and have an excellent conversation with Dr. Jose Salazar about these physical changes. Here again, we see the importance of developing good working relationships with your veterinarian.

Everyone ages: people, pets, anything or anyone living. Our bodies all change, and, with those changes, conditions related to the aging process can appear gradually or quickly. Dr. Salazar confirmed it was normal changes related to aging that were affecting Wookie's joints, causing the beginning stages of arthritis and degeneration. He recommended we try injection medication to improve her mobility. We could bring her to the office and have the techs give her the shot, or they could teach me how to administer it myself at home. Because we lived about ten miles from the clinic, I was all about learning to give her the shots myself at home. I wanted to be able to take care her myself, if possible. The techs graciously showed me how, and I went home and started to administer her injections. She learned to relax for me while sitting on my lap, and by her actions it was apparent she could sense I was trying to help and take care of her, and she trusted me. She did not squawk or squirm, and all went well. Afterwards, she often gave me her sweet little Wookie smile and a gentle kiss. I only had to administer the shot when she really needed it, which I did in accordance with the medication instructions. In time, Wookie improved significantly, and I rarely had to give her the shot at all. But it was a personal wakeup call to me she was indeed getting older.

While many pet owners choose a veterinarian and stick to the most basic interactions possible—simply asking about the needed shots and coming in for the occasional routine checkup—it's important to take things to the next level, just as I did when I started having new concerns about Wookie's overall well-being and health. You need to develop a partnership and fully engage with your vet, so you can effectively team with them in giving the best care possible. It can be very scary when your pet is in critical need of care and you don't have an established relationship with a trusted vet.

The first step in building that trust is establishing an open line of communication. Work on building rapport and do not be afraid to ask the questions you need and want to ask. Go beyond the basics and make sure your vet knows all your concerns. This might make you uncomfortable at first, but it is crucial you step out of your comfort zone. This is the person who you are trusting to care for the health of your pet. They are there to help you. Ask the hard questions whenever you have an opportunity to do so: there inevitably will come a time when they will need to be answered.

A good vet won't mind talking through your questions and concerns. In fact, they appreciate and value your concerns. They will let you weigh the options and consequences for your pet and yourself carefully. While living in California, when I found that lump on Wookie's neck, Dr. Block recommended surgery to remove it. Wookie was ten years old, and I was worried she would have difficulty going through such a procedure. I wanted to know what I should expect. I asked if surgery was advisable at her age. Dr. Block acknowledged Wookie was older, but explained she was also very healthy and should have no problems with the surgery or recovery. Of course, because it was cancer being removed, there was always a possibility it could return in the future, with no guarantees. But it was still worth doing the surgery, and her life expectancy improved with the removal of the tumor. With this reassurance, I could decide on the best course of action, feeling confident and informed.

Sometimes, it's best to simply ask, "If this was your pet, what would you do?" I asked that very question of Dr. Quillivan, who cared for Wookie when her seizures were occurring, and her answer helped guide me to the EOL decision I ultimately made.

Granted, trusting your vet does not mean you automatically must do exactly what they recommend. Always ask for all possible available options and alternatives on medications and procedures, etc. You are your pet's strongest advocate. Good information empowers good decisions. It helps to have the input and advice of someone else who is both knowledgeable and invested in your pet's best interests, but, ultimately, the decisions fall to you. You must be proactive and willing to gather as much information as possible so you can make the best decisions.

FACING HARD DECISIONS

Having a strong relationship with your vet helps most

during difficult and stressful situations. Knowing you can rely on your vet can make the tough times more bearable. Facing illness, an accident, or the possibility of having to euthanize your pet is hard enough without having a trained professional as part of your support system. You need to feel confident in making the important decisions and know the vet is in your corner.

If your pet is older and needs surgery, you must consider the fact it will need a great deal of aftercare and likely have decreased energy for a while. When Wookie had her cancer surgery, she was extremely tired afterward. It took a lot of out of her, more than I imagined it would. I was lucky to be able to be home with her during the recovery period. I took everything off my plate and was there with her. I gave her lots of TLC. She had no idea why she was weak or slow with otherwise routine mobility. She did not understand it all. It mattered not. I was her devoted companion and took care of her. She had been my cuddle buddy and stayed close beside me when I had double knee surgery. She stuck like glue to Aaron when he had shoulder surgery and was Randy's constant companion by his side when he was in recovery from his cancer surgery. She sensed in all cases that we needed extra love and her companionship. She did not want us to feel bad. Wookie's presence was very soothing and beneficial to our well-being and recovery. Such devotion and unconditional love from our beloved pets is very potent medicine for us all. It was easy to be there for her and provide comfort when she needed it after her surgery. What goes around, comes around.

If surgery is recommended for your pet, you will need to consider many things. What will you do if you need to work? Will you have to consider in-home care? What if your pet will never be the same? It can be tempting to answer such questions based primarily on your emotions rather than professional advice. A good vet will help you navigate those feelings and come to the best possible decision for you and your pet at the time. These are important decisions you have to make not only for your pet, but for yourself and your family.

The same is true when euthanasia is being considered. When Wookie had her seizures, I asked Dr. Quillivan about getting more tests. She could tell I was getting emotional and helped me to regain my composure, then think rationally. I had always told myself that, when the time came, I wanted to be able to let Wookie go with dignity. Her QOL was most important. I didn't want her to struggle, have diminished capacity, or feel pain. By encouraging me to slow down and think clearly, my vet helped me see the right choice for myself, my family, and Wookie.

In this respect, veterinarians carry an enormous responsibility unique to their field. It is the only occupation that allows for total control over life and death. The weight of that responsibility is immense, and those who chose veterinary medicine as a career must shoulder it daily. The reality of compassion fatigue is very real in their profession, along with other pet caregivers in many capacities.

Therefore, it is important that we, as pet owners, fully understand and appreciate this reality within the animal care profession. Our veterinary staff and others need our ongoing support, appreciation, and compassion. They also need to recognize the adverse effects of compassion fatigue as it affects them personally.

LISTEN, THEN DECIDE

A number of vets I have spoken with said that, while they are always willing to dispense the best professional advice possible, they always leave the final decision with the pet owner. There can be a wide array of circumstances at play affecting the decision. I know a family who, due to various circumstances, had limited financial means at the time their dog was hit by a car. The accident caused significant injury to the dog's hip. He needed surgery, which would cost several thousand dollars, plus multiple medications and perhaps rehabilitation.

The family had to weigh the options carefully. If the surgery wasn't performed, the dog would die. But they knew they were uncomfortable shouldering the burden of the high costs at that time. They struggled immensely with the decision, but in the end, felt they only had one choice. They had to let their dog go.

On the other hand, there are times when people let their emotions take over completely and make costly decisions they cannot realistically afford. I recently read an interesting article about a woman who had a dog who needed surgery. She asked her vet's opinion, and he advised against it, explaining the dog likely would not live much longer regardless. She went forward with it, spending over $30,000, and the dog lived only a short period after the surgery, then died. She still lost her companion and, in the process, took on a deep, pinching financial obligation. It helps to think ahead about what you would do in similar emotional situations so you can make the best overall choices.

Pet owners also must weigh the advice of their vets, then make their own intelligent and prudent decisions, especially with respect to their own personal situations and circumstances. Don't allow your emotions to be your only guide. Remember that what you feel is best for you is not always or necessarily the best option for your pet. The QOL, the ongoing care, and the dignity of your pet must be considered as well.

WHEN RELATIONSHIPS ARE RUSHED

Even when you've spent a significant amount of time building rapport with your vet, changes and the unexpected can happen. Your pet might become ill when you are traveling, or your regular vet might be on vacation when an emergency arises. No matter what the case, you must still handle the situation at hand and be able to communicate with the attending vet who is caring for your pet.

The most important thing you can do in these situations is talk. When you don't know the vet in charge of caring for your pet companion, start getting to know them and communicate. Ask the questions you need to ask to make the best decisions. Encourage the vet to tell you everything possible about the scenario you're facing. What options do you have? What will your pet be like after surgery? What is to be expected, and what does aftercare look like? What are the best and worst-case scenarios? What kind of pain will the pet be in, and will the QOL decline? Do whatever you can to keep the communication going until you feel fully informed and ready to decide.

If you are struggling to make a concrete decision, take time to think. Step away and breathe. Be clear and tell the vet, "I'm having a difficult time with this decision. I'm very emotional. I'm afraid to make the wrong decision." Very likely, the vet will respond by saying, "Let's give you a little more time so you're comfortable with the path forward." They might recommend you take your pet home and think about it, watch how your pet is doing, and come back in a few days, barring no imminent concerns while your pet is home, resting. Call them if you have questions or if things worsen. But it is also important to understand that taking your pet home as you consider their EOL options can be very stressful. It's hard to watch anyone we love when they are in pain or ill, but sometimes it is what we need to do to see the situation more clearly.

I had never met Dr. Quillivan before the day we had to euthanize Wookie. I had been to the other of her two clinics multiple times, and had a great rapport with the staff, especially Dr. Salazar. It would have been easier if we had had him in our time of need, but that does not always happen. We need to be prepared in all medical-related scenarios for our pets. Because of the high level of quality care I had always received for Wookie at the day clinic, I felt comfortable and that I could trust Dr. Quillivan. It made it easier to communicate with her, and, as previously noted, her guidance in that extremely stressful situation proved invaluable.

When we decided to proceed with euthanizing Wookie while together in the examination room, Dr. Quillivan did one of the best and most touching things she could have possibly done. She gently and sweetly rubbed Wookie, then looked up at us and smiled lightly. She said, "You made the best decision for Wookie." That's the bottom line. You need to make the best decision you can as a pet owner. When you don't know what to do, you need to look to the people who have years of experience in these situations. Allow them to offer advice. They will be honest and open with you about what your pet is dealing with and what they believe is best in the situation. Listen. Hear what they have to say. They are there to support you and help you through what you're facing. It is their job. Then, it's up to you to make the best decision.

It's the nature of being a veterinarian to deal with both life and death. What's important is that they do so with compassion and understanding for the animals and their families, and guide their clients, the pet owners, to make important QOL and EOL decisions accordingly,

WORKING WITH YOUR CLINIC

The relationship you build with your vet should extend to their staff as well. They are all part of your support system. When you notice them taking an extra measure to care for you and your pet, make sure you let them know how much you appreciate them and positively acknowledge the service rendered.

Just as you would do with your physician's office, it's important to let your vet know when anything has changed with your pet. This helps them stay up-to-date and able to best serve you and your pet. Whether it's a call to let them know you're moving or your pet's health has changed, it's important to make sure you communicate any change.

It's also important to treat all clinic staff with the proper respect and, again, acknowledge their good works. In high-stress scenarios, people often negatively take their frustrations out on others, especially the attending staff. Remember the staff is there to help you, not to add to an already painful situation. Just as anger can beget anger, kindness begets kindness. When you show thankfulness and appreciation, that kindness is reciprocated positively forward.

We have become acquainted with and are very fond of Wookie's boarding tech, Brittany, and when our puppy girl passed away, she took the time to send us a card and silver picture frame with a photo she'd taken of Wookie. The frame has "memories" written across the top and sends that message clearly and sweetly to everyone who sees it. This photo is nestled together with other family photos of the kids and grandkids. Wookie was indeed a special part of our family. Her spot is reserved right there next to other family members, both those living and those who have passed on.

The rapport we'd built with Brittany had come back to us as a gesture of kindness, and it came when we needed it most. I invited her over for lunch to show our appreciation, and we simply spent time together. We had a lovely time and got to know each other better in the process, as a friendship was forged.

Compassion in action pays forward with dividends of love.

Tough Decisions

EUTHANASIA AND ENDING CARE

Euthanasia is the last give of love.
—DR. KIM EATON, DVM

No matter what kind of pet you have or how long you've had it, when faced with the possibility of euthanasia, you will feel guilt. Even when you know in your heart it is the right decision, and there is no other path forward, second-guessing and heartache are inevitable. It's a substantial weight for anyone to bear, but it is also a natural part of the process when you decide to let your pet go with dignity.

WHAT IS EUTHANASIA?

Euthanasia is the process of giving excess amounts of anesthetic drugs with the intent to end life. The word "euthanasia" comes from the two Greek words: "eu," which means good, and "thanatos," which means death. Therefore, euthanasia translates as "good death."

The actual process begins with a pet owner and veterinarian discussing that this may be needed when a pet is suffering. It is important to discuss your pet's QOL with a veterinarian so information is gathered and shared to make the best decision for both you and your pet. Some pet owners seem to "just know" when it is time, because their pet has lost interest in normal activities, eating, or being with other members of the family. For many pet owners, the decision is more difficult. It is not a decision you have to make on your own. Talk to your veterinarian to get more information about QOL assessment.

The actual procedure consists of giving the pet an excess amount of anesthetic agents. Anesthesia comes from more Greek words, "an," meaning without, and "aesthesis," meaning sensation. Anesthetics take away all sensation by creating a state of unconsciousness. As an excess amount is given, the brain and heart also lose sensation and stop functioning.

Veterinarians may have different anesthetics and procedures for performing euthanasia. It is important to ask your veterinarian what to expect and what will happen during euthanasia. Sometimes, a sedative is given to calm the pet while an intravenous catheter is placed. The anesthetic drugs are very often given directly into the bloodstream via this catheter. Anesthetics are rapidly acting medications that will cause anesthesia. This is a painless, peaceful, and swift process used to prevent suffering.

–DR. JESSICA QUILLIVAN, DVM

It should also be noted that many vets perform euthanasia slightly differently for different pets in different situations. With this in mind, it is extremely important to encourage each and every pet owner to discuss all aspects of their pet's individual circumstances. There could be a variation to the euthanasia procedure selected in their particular situation. Open and frank discussion will dispel and eliminate confusion. All pet owners want to understand exactly what to expect. Please take the time to talk and listen as your vet explains the specific procedure recommended for your pet family member.

DIFFERENT PEOPLE, DIFFERENT PLACES

My first exposure to euthanasia came when I was living in California. I was sitting in the waiting room of Dr. Block's office with Wookie when I noticed another family holding their dog and crying. I couldn't help but reach out to them. They explained they had started conversations with the vet about the possibility of euthanasia for their pet and had reached their EOL decision. They told me they were taking their dog home to say goodbye. I could feel the sorrow radiating from their hearts as the situation pulled their emotions in every direction. I witnessed their anticipatory grief as they struggled with the knowledge that their last moments with their pet companion were soon approaching.

I didn't know what to say or how to comfort them. My heart was broken. These were people I didn't know, but I couldn't help but hurt for them.

Shortly thereafter, when Wookie was having surgery to remove the cancer, I experienced a similar situation. While sitting in the waiting area in Dr. Block's office, I could hear a woman sobbing in another room. I spoke with the receptionist to inquire if the woman was okay. She explained the family had just euthanized their pet. Some people around me in the waiting room started to become a bit uneasy. I watched several of them grow antsy in their chairs, some getting up and walking away to distance themselves from what was happening. They wanted to push it away or ignore it. Such reactions saddened me, as I realized this family needed compassion now more than ever. Dealing firsthand with death and loss is never easy and can often make others uncomfortable.

Everyone responds to euthanasia differently, and much of their response is based on their past experiences with it. Those who have gone through loss and grief usually are able to empathize and show compassion. Others who haven't often struggle to understand the pain of losing a pet. They push away the reality of what's going on. Their reactions, which stem from a lack of understanding, are not intentionally harmful, but they can be upsetting to the people experiencing the pain. Perhaps this is because they know they will one day soon be in the same scenario with their pet. No one wants to think about that dreadful day.

When Wookie's surgery ended, and she was resting, I spoke with the vet about what I had witnessed. She said while euthanasia is a difficult reality of her profession, guiding families through the process is always extremely important, although very hard. She explained that every circumstance and situation is unique, and every family must deal with it in their own way. She said her team tries to give these families privacy and allow them all the time they need with their pet so they can say goodbye.

This made me think about the two sides of euthanasia I'd seen: first, watching the family as they anticipated the loss of their pet, then later seeing the grief and pain of another family just after they'd lost theirs. Everyone deals with it differently, but we all feel pain when we lose someone we love, and we deserve to be treated with respect, care, and kindness.

Dr. Quillivan remarked in her definition of euthanasia that: "Veterinarians may have different anesthetics and procedures for performing euthanasia." While euthanasia is most commonly performed in the veterinary clinic, some veterinarians perform the act, which Dr. Kim Eaton (my son Doug's neighbor and veterinarian) calls "the last gift of love," in the pet owner's home.

I was recently talking with a group of ladies at a neighborhood gathering, when the topic of pets came up. I asked my friend, Ali, about the story of her precious Greta and was very touched. Greta loved her pet owners, Ali and John, to the max. She was gentle-natured and loved to wander around the house getting lots of affection from everyone and just being a part of simple everyday life with her family and friends. The dog especially loved it when Ali's granddaughter, Paige, came to see them. The child loved Greta and developed a special relationship with her grandma's pooch. Just as my grandchildren did with Wookie, Greta knew Paige was part of her family, too.

When Ali told me that Greta lived to be "fifteen years and seven months old," it struck me as so touching: she knew to the exact month how long they shared life with their sweet companion. Greta was not gravely ill, as was the case with some of the other pet stories I have previously shared or will share, but the big issue was her QOL. She was showing the normal effects of simply getting older. That time-stealer, old age, was taking its toll, just as it does with every two-legged or four-legged being in the end. Greta's gait became slower, and her sleeping increased dramatically. In the end, "accidents" happened, and diapers were sometimes used.

The family saw her waning and knew her QOL and health were declining and diminishing. Every pet owner hates to see this and knows what is coming next. Ali discussed Greta's condition with Dr. Quillivan and shared her concerns.

Because Greta did not have any serious, life-threatening disease, Ali simply asked the vet to "let them know when it was time." Ali admits she "kind of knew it was time," but told Dr. Quillivan just to tell her when. Sometimes, we need to actually hear those words from a doctor who shares a relationship with both parties, the client and the patient.

When Dr. Quillivan told them it was time, Ali knew it, too. Even still, who wants to let go of a dedicated and precious pet? The answer is absolutely no one! But there are definitely times when the correct answer is, "It is time to let go." Ali also admits they probably allowed Greta to continue her life a few months more than they really should have. This is not uncommon. When we love so deeply, we cannot imagine letting go. And when we do, we cannot imagine how we are going to continue our normal routines without our pets.

But this is where the last gift we give our companion is the compassion to let them go in peace. The QOL is that important. It is not fair to expect them to experience life with diminished capacity, immobility, pain, or degeneration.

Ali and John wanted to have Greta's euthanasia performed at their home. They felt more comfortable with that decision, and Dr. Quillivan came and provided their last gift of love in their home. If this is something you have time to plan and prepare for, you might want to inquire if your vet is willing to do this.

COMPASSION IN HEALING

Compassion is powerful and, in many situations, necessary. Families who lose their pets need the compassion of others, just as the animal needs compassion from its family when it is time to let go.

It's natural to want to hold on to a loved one for as long as possible, but sometimes ending the animal's suffering is the most compassionate solution for both the pet and pet owner. This concept was best described to me by Dr. Eaton, who calls euthanasia "the last gift of love." To me, this is a beautiful way to think about such a painful situation. When your pet companion is suffering, allowing them to be at peace can be the final way you show them how much you care.

This is how I choose to think about our decision to let Wookie go. I remember her last moments. The seizures were battling her small body, and I knew it was not right to make her endure any more pain. At the time, I clung to the hope I could bring her home one last time, but, looking back, I am thankful I didn't. If she'd gone into a seizure again at home, it would have been too hard for all of us. As Dr. Quillivan explained, Wookie wasn't herself anymore. She didn't know us, and she didn't know herself. That's not the way our beloved pet should live. That's not dignity or good QOL. We knew we were making the right and best decision when we chose to proceed with euthanizing her. It was hard, and it hurt me, but we knew we were loving her and showing her compassion.

Letting Wookie go also meant we could let go. We could begin to heal. The agony of her physical death was over, she was no longer in pain, and now, we could start our grief journey with the understanding we did what was best for our pet.

THINKING BEYOND OURSELVES

The most important thing you can do when considering euthanasia is to put your own emotions and fears aside and ask what is best for the animal. What is the reality of your pet's condition? What will their QOL be? Are you pushing to keep your pet alive for its sake or for yours? Do you want to be able to look back on the situation and say, "I kept him around too long," or "I know I made the best decision I could for him"? Will this likely become a decision you must revisit in the very near future? If so, recognize your grief will be just as bad in a couple months as it will be right now.

This is another reason communication with the vet is so important. You must ask all the questions you can to get a clear sense of the situation. Find out whether your pet's health is likely to improve with treatment, or if treatment will simply prolong life with complications. Consider if the pet has nothing to look forward to but pain and limited mobility, and what their QOL will be.

It helps to seek consultation from loved ones, whether it be your spouse, children, or other family or friends who will also be directly impacted by the loss, provided there is enough time to do so. Other times, the choice must be made quickly. Either way, the vet is there to support your decision and give you the best advice possible. They want you to be comfortable in the choice you make. The choice is yours; you must make it.

KNOW WHAT TO EXPECT

If euthanasia is the best option, then allow your vet the opportunity to fully explain the procedure and what to expect. Surprises and misunderstandings can be even harder in difficult circumstances.

After we had time to say goodbye to Wookie, Dr. Quillivan was very kind and gracious about telling us what to expect. She said, "She's been sedated. She's ready. She's calm. She's not going to feel anything. When I put the medication into the IV, she will become unconscious, and her heart will stop. It's swift and peaceful."

She also explained that, in some cases, the animal could possibly have a muscular reaction that results in movement of their limbs. The pet is already gone, but occasionally a natural muscle spasm occurs. I was so grateful she told us about that, because had Wookie experienced that, I might have thought she was in pain. It would have been traumatic and added to an already painful situation.

Decide if you want to spend time with your pet during the euthanasia procedure or afterward. Perhaps neither. For some people, this just is too painful. For others, it offers a sense of closure to remain with their pet for a period or during the procedure itself. The choice is yours. It has to be whatever makes you most comfortable. No one decision is the right one for everyone: at this point, you must do what is best for you.

You also will have to think about what you want to happen after your pet is gone. How do you wish to handle the remains? It is an important and very personal decision. If you are considering taking your pet home and burying it on your property, review applicable local ordinances and think about what you'd like to transport them home in. Some people choose to bring their pet's favorite blanket to wrap them in, as it's a comfort to see them covered in something they enjoyed. Talk to your vet about other ideas, have the discussion together, and ask what other families have done to show extra care for their pets.

MONEY MATTERS

Sometimes financial circumstances impact our decisions related to caring for our pets. Deciding to stop treatment because you cannot afford it can lead to a great deal of agonizing. However, if paying the cost of a treatment is going to put you or your family in a compromising financial situation, you might need to decide to forgo it. It saddens the heart, but it is a reality that needs to be considered very seriously.

You might have to take time off from work to care for a pet after a complicated surgery. You might need to consider in-home services to help with recovery. Even then, you must ask: what is the projected longevity for your pet? Even with such extended care, life expectancy might be short. Such factors can significantly impact your finances and should be considered carefully.

If money is a major factor for you or your family, talk to the vet about the cost of your pet's treatment. Weigh the value of the treatment against the cost. Can you afford the right treatment in the first place? Will your pet be healthier and have a better QOL after the treatment is complete? If you don't ask these questions before you make your decision, you risk putting yourself in a compromising financial situation you can't afford.

BRINGING YOUR PET HOME: CONTEMPLATING EOL

As previously discussed, you can bring your sick or debilitated pet home with your vet's approval while you consider if euthanasia is your best choice. This idea is very important. You must consider the related ramifications to make the best decision. It is one way many people begin to cope with the inevitable loss of their companion. However, doing so can evoke feelings of anticipatory grief at the pet's probable near-future death. We want to postpone the pain, yet often we find we have invited even more in when we prolong the situation.

The decision to take the pet home for a few days to think things through or to say goodbye becomes more complicated when there are children involved. Your pet might be experiencing the debilitative effects of their illness or injury, and the family will experience every moment of their pain with them. If you have children, you must think about the challenge they will face in trying to understand why their pet has to die soon, especially when they realize their parents have to make a decision about euthanasia. Also consider how bringing the pet home will affect your other pets and how those other pets will behave. These other cherished pets in our home are very intuitive and understand perhaps even more than we give them credit for. There are so many things to consider. Ultimately, you must make the best decision for yourself and your family, and as your pet's advocate.

None of us want to let go of a family member, whether they're human or animal. They are part of our lives. We love them. We feel the absence when they're gone.

We know animals' lives are short. While it's not pleasant to realize death and loss are a part of living, there comes a time when we all must face that reality. It helps to think about these difficult scenarios ahead of time and plan for when the tough decisions must be made.

As in my friend Patty's case, bringing her companion Buffy home for a final weekend to say goodbye enabled her and her husband Don time to jointly confirm the path forward to euthanasia, to understand together that "it was time." Patty was happy they had these last moments with Buffy.

Hard as it was, it helped them better come to grips with what was impending.

Everyone is different and handles things differently. No matter the choice, for one last time at home together or not, associated anticipatory grief is real and difficult. But bringing our pet home can possibly enable us to better understand the process and what can be expected.

Your Pet's Remains and Effects

If there are no dogs in heaven, then when
I die, I want to go where they went.

—WILL ROGERS

Many people don't realize how many options there are for handling pet remains. While your vet can explain the options, and help you make the best decision for you and your family, it is ultimately up to you to decide what you are most comfortable with.

BURIAL

Many pet owners opt to bury their animals, either on their own property or in designated pet cemeteries.

Your vet can refer you to a cemetery where you can have your pet laid to rest. Some are like regular cemeteries and have plots dedicated to each pet. Others are less personal; these are called group cemeteries.

You also can also bury your pet on your own property. There are several factors to consider when doing so. What will happen if you move? Is there local wildlife that could disrupt the grave site? Be aware of any county or city regulations and ordinances that apply to a burial on your property. It's important to consider your environment when making decisions about burial sites.

CREMATION

Cremation is another common option, and the one we chose for Wookie. Some pet owners like to keep their companions' ashes in an urn or a specially selected container of their choice. Some prefer to spread their pet's ashes on their own property. If you are interested in spreading the ashes in a public place, it is important you check to make sure the area allows for it, as some do not. Some places have ordinances in place that carry hefty fines when disobeyed.

Should you opt for a container, there are many ways to make it more personalized and special. You can get everything from beautiful boxes and unique ornate containers to small, simple urns. You can inscribe a name or message on them, depending on your preference. For Wookie, we chose a small carved wooden box with a silver plate that we had engraved to say, "Wookie, Our Puppy Girl." We keep it in our home office, and while it was difficult initially to have the ashes so close by, it now gives me comfort. When I go in the office, I get the sense she's still with us, and it brings me peace. It's all about personal preference.

When I picked up Wookie's contained ashes, a "molded small paw print" with her name inscribed across the top was also included, sitting in a small black holder. This was an unexpected surprise and touching memento included with her ashes. Today, it graces my bookshelves in our office beside a photo of her.

MEMORIAL GARDEN

Some people commemorate their pets by mixing their ashes in soil to make a little garden or plant a tree.

A friend of mine who lost her daughter keeps her ashes in a memorial garden we helped build. She tends to the garden regularly, and it serves as a soothing way for her to honor her daughter and celebrate her life.

A memorial garden can celebrate the life of your pet in the same way. It turns sadness into something beautiful and helps ease the pain of the loss in a very healthy way.

MEMORIAL SERVICE

A memorial service can provide a sense of closure and serve as an important step in the healing process. There are no limits to how you can celebrate your pet's life. Some people write poems or release balloons. Others write letters to their pets, expressing their love and deep sentiments, or light candles. For each person, "memorial" means something different, so think about what would be the most meaningful thing for you, your family members, and friends who were close to your pet. It can be very comforting to children in the family, rather like sentimental therapy and an outward expression of the love everyone shared for their lost companion.

For my Wookie, several kids wrote letters. Our family still often refer to and talk about sweet memories of her. In our case, sharing emotions promoted healing. She was an important part of our entire family for many years and lives on through our memories. Wookie still holds a special place within our hearts.

No matter what you do, the important thing is to be there for each other, acknowledge the loss, and move forward on your journey to recovery.

PRAYER

Prayer can be helpful if it is already part of your life. If you desire to now incorporate prayer into your life, feel free to do so. It might help to soothe and soften your grief and pain. I found it helped me enormously throughout my grief. Sometimes, it helps to bring your family together to pray. It allows you to find comfort in your support for each other. Faith and prayer can be strong and soothing components in the healing process and soften the pain of loss.

For each person, healing means something different. Whether it happens through a memorial service or garden, a personalized urn, spreading the ashes someplace special, or burying your pet in a favorite place, there is no right answer. No one size fits all. Whatever the healing process entails for you, find a way to celebrate your pet's life. Do what you need to so you can find peace and closure.

HANDLING YOUR PET'S EFFECTS

When you are grieving, one of the first things that demands your attention is your pet's effects. You don't want to immediately discard everything, but, at the same time, keeping certain things for too long could possibly stall your healing. You will have no need of open medications, vitamins, and hygiene products, such as lotions, creams, shampoo, etc. Unopened medicine and hygiene products might be able to be given away to someone you know who could use them. Sharing is an opportunity to care and heal. You might know of someone who would put the remaining pet food products to use.

When Wookie died, the first thing I did was gather all her belongings together. I knew that seeing them every day would make the grief worse for me. I separated items I could share with others who could use them and put away what I could, but I didn't throw anything away initially. I simply wanted to be able to share what Wookie left behind.

If you're tempted to start throwing everything away, especially favorite toys and so on, I'd advise you to wait. Give yourself some time. When you first come home from losing a pet, you're very emotional. You might find your-self wishing later you'd kept certain things—their collar, stuffed animals, or toys; often simple, everyday items—as mementos. Such items are precious and cannot be replaced once gone.

Again, if you really feel driven to eliminate something, get rid of opened pills or chewed-up toys that can't be saved. If you have things you can share, such as food or bedding, contact your friends, or call your vet or local shelter to find out how you can donate them. This is both a way of cele-brating your pet's life and a way of taking care of yourself while "paying it forward."

BE CAREFUL WITH ROUTINES

While everyone must grieve in their own way, in their own time, continuing a routine after your pet is gone might do your emotions more harm than good. When you keep non-memento items around, such as shampoo, food, or medicine, you might be avoiding the reality of what's happened. Sharing is caring and a positive action toward recovery. Sometimes people who struggle to let go con-tinue to put food and water in their pets' bowls. I am not a medical professional, but in doing research I have found allowing such habits to continue could possibly keep you from beginning to heal. We want to positively press forward and not cling to the past. It cannot be brought back. The here and now offers a new beginning, an opportunity to heal and mend your broken heart.

By continuing to leave your pet's bed where it's always been for too long, you are reminded that your pet isn't there to sleep in it every time you pass by it. By not putting away food and water bowls, you're leaving them there to be seen countless times each day. And each time, this brings pain. It could possibly stunt and slow the healing process and, in a way, keep you from moving forward. We all cope in our own unique way, but I urge you to focus on doing things that promote positive growth and healing. Everyone is different, but, with time, we all will heal.

You want to allow yourself to begin to heal. You want the heart to mend. Yes, your environment is going to be different: your pet is no longer there with you and that means many things are going to change. You're not going to hear the jingle of their collar or precious purring, or see them sitting in their favorite spot or in their stall in the barn. You will miss the sound of the song they serenaded you with. No amount of "stuff" you keep will bring them back. Instead, it's important to focus on the memories and special mementos, and keep them alive in your mind and heart.

MEMENTOS THAT HEAL

When you find the one, two, or however many mementos that are really significant to you, use them to help you hold onto the joyful memories. It might be a much-loved toy or blanket. For me, it was Wookie's collar, elf suit, a few stuffed toys, and, of course, her tennis ball.

I wanted to do something special with her collar, so I set it aside and later placed it on our holiday tree. As a family, we enjoy celebrating Christmas together. It is a very meaningful, religious time filled with family traditions, decorations, and a special tree. Our Christmas tree tradition started years ago, when I would decorate it with family mementos, ornaments, and items our kids made when they were young. Twenty-five years ago, I decided to place a special stuffed Winnie the Pooh Bear on the tree, which I purchased in London when Randy and I celebrated our twentieth anniversary there. It still evokes those special memories we shared together. Over the years, our tree has become adorned with a unique collection of teddy bears I've collected from all over the world. I found a ceramic schnauzer ornament in Williamsburg the Thanksgiving holiday weekend we spent there with our son, Doug, and his family shortly after we lost Wookie. It looks just like Wookie! When I showed it to Randy, he suggested I put it on the tree next to Wookie's collar. I did, and now every time we look at it, we are filled with happiness and fond memories. The collar and schnauzer ornament evoke precious memories of her and that special day in Williamsburg we shared with Doug's family. When the kids come for the holidays, they look for her collar and the schnauzer ornament.

This is just one way we keep Wookie as a part of our lives and remember the joy she brought. No matter how you choose to honor or remember your pet, allow it to be part of your own healing process.

Grieving Is Normal

Grief is the price we pay for love.
—QUEEN ELIZABETH II

The grief we feel when we lose a pet is real and completely normal. When we lose someone we love, we feel broken in places we didn't even know we had. Regardless of social standing, age, or celebrity status, we all have broken hearts when we lose someone we love.

I was very touched by the public expressions of grief two celebrities showed after the loss of their pets. In 2017, Barbra Streisand posted a tribute on Instagram to her beloved dog Samantha, who died at age fourteen. She shared the last photo taken of her and Samantha together and captioned the photo, "May she rest in peace. We cherish every moment of the 14 years we had with her. May 2003 – May 2017."

The actor Tom Hardy rescued his dog, Woodstock, when he spotted him running across a busy roadway in Atlanta. When "Woody" died in 2017 at just six years old, his heart-broken owner wrote a tribute to the animal that was posted on the fan site Tom Hardy Dot Org. "It is with great, great sadness, a heavy heart that I inform you that after a very hard and short 6-month battle with an aggressive Polymyositis, Woody passed away," Hardy wrote.

Even with many people talking publicly about pet loss, sometimes we feel alone in our sadness, as though no one else has ever felt the way we do. We might question why we are feeling the way we feel. There are several factors contributing to this sense of isolation.

OWNING THE UNEXPECTED

Loss of a pet is often sudden and unexpected. With little to no time to prepare, you might feel left in a lurch for some time afterward. For me, the pendulum swing of going from vacation mode to losing Wookie was jarring. We had been away, enjoying our time with family in Colorado, and never expected to come home and lose her within twenty-four hours.

While I felt isolated in that pain, what I experienced was no different than someone else who has lost. Barbara, whose little Lukie escaped from his leash and was hit by a truck, endured a loss that was equally unexpected and painful. Miller, who lost her beloved riding companion Red when the back of her trailer unexpectedly swerved, never anticipated saying goodbye so soon. Losing four beloved pet companions and her home to the ravages of wildfire also carried significant grief and heart-wrenching loss for Rose.

Losing pets in the devastation of any type of natural disaster, such as flood, hurricane, or tornado, is equally painful. It is a reality and unfortunate part of our existence on this earth. It is important to understand this unique kind of loss.

DISASTERS, DEVASTATION, AND LOSS: LESSONS LEARNED FROM HARVEY

When we lose to natural disasters, the devastation is typically swift, unexpected, and often of epic proportions. Disasters are often much more complicated losses that affect all aspects of human existence and everyday life. The most difficult loss is when family members are involved, both two-legged and four-legged. A significant number of people and pets become injured, die, or are lost and never recovered as a result of natural disasters. The experience of this kind of loss is deepened when it is coupled with the loss of personal effects and property.

Living in Texas, I have become familiar with the devastation hurricanes, tropical storms, and storm surges can bring. I have seen it firsthand, experienced it myself, and worked as a volunteer in disaster recovery. It is heartbreaking to the max.

In September 2008, Hurricane Ike, a Category 2, ravaged our community and eighty-seven other surrounding counties. Our home was badly damaged: our roof had to be repaired and re-shingled, there was interior water leakage, our gate and fence were demolished, and the grandkids' jungle gym and swing set were destroyed. We had no power for two weeks in near-100-degree temperatures. Our portable generator failed, along with a friend's small backup generator, and we lost all our refrigerated foods. Mangled trees sprawled across the landscape, and large blue plastic tarps covered roofs.

Thousands of people lost loved ones and everything they owned, making the property damage we sustained seem minuscule. We truly considered ourselves extremely blessed and lucky comparatively. Homes and properties can be rebuilt, but we can never get back the people or pets we lose. Yet even in the midst of disaster, whether it be a hurricane, tornado, wildfire, tsunami, flood, earthquake, or other natural event, we have to forge ahead and face our grief.

In August 2017, Texas and Louisiana once again sustained another major catastrophic hit with Hurricane Harvey, a Category 4. Harvey has been recorded as one of the worst all- time storms in American history. Thousands upon thousands of people and animals of all kinds were adversely affected.

Because our home is on high ground, we did not see anywhere near the level of devastation with Harvey as we did with our loses from Ike. From safety, we watched on the news as thousands of people struggled to escape the rising flood waters. Many carried their pets to safety, while so many more were forced to abandon and leave their beloved companions behind.

Thankfully, there are a vast number of dedicated compassionate animal rescue organizations and volunteers specifically assisting with pet recovery efforts. It is possible for a rescued pet to be reunited with its family, but those chances become slimmer and slimmer as time passes. More than likely, if a pet is lucky enough to be rescued and saved, it will be transported and sheltered initially at a new location. Some animals rescued from Harvey were flown directly to other states, where they were adopted by new families. We all wish and hope the best for these rescued animals, and are extremely grateful to the kindhearted people who have saved them from harm.

With this in mind, I encourage all pet owners to have their pets *microchipped*. It is one way to give yourself a better possibility, even if it's remote, of recovering a lost pet and being reunited with your animal if saved and rescued.

WHAT IS A MICROCHIP IMPLANT?

A microchip implant, or "chip," is a detector inserted under the animal's skin, which can be scanned at a shelter or vet's office to help an owner locate the animal when lost.

For families who are not able to reunite with their pets, not knowing whether they are safe or not can be unbearable. The pain, anguish, and sorrow are overwhelming beyond measure. This kind of loss is probably among the most difficult to overcome and will take a significant amount of time and patience to recover from.

In these times, it is so important to put our faith, compassion, and caring into action, and appreciate the love and support of others. We must appreciate our special blessings and be grateful that we are alive and have survived. Then, we can elect to endure, pressing positively forward. This is a choice we have the power to make within ourselves. No one can do it for us. We have control over our attitude and feelings.

The unexpected is and will always be part of life. It is why we say, "Expect the unexpected." We can't control any of it, but we can decide how we react. We have power over what we do and how we bring ourselves back from heartache.

A SPECIAL KIND OF LOVE

Another factor complicating our feelings is the unique relationship between pet owner and pet companion. It is very different and unique unto itself, compared to the relationships you often experience with people. Outside of your immediate family, the pet might be the closest relationship you have. Of course, you love your extended family, but perhaps you don't see each other very often. Human relationships can be extremely complex and often strained by a multitude of factors, such as distance, personalities, differences, disputes, and an endless list of other scenarios.

My friend Kathleen had a very special companion, her cat Dice. He had always been there for her with his special, unconditional love, helping her each day to navigate through her adventures of life, the good times and trying days, too. Her cat was social by nature, very friendly and giving, especially to his beloved Kathleen. Dice was a great pal and confidant, in spite of some special needs of his own. He was diagnosed with feline AIDS, which can adversely affect lung function. No matter what, Kathleen always did her best to love, support, and care for him and his special needs, just as he tried to reciprocate this affection.

One evening, Kathleen came home from work excited and expecting to be warmly greeted by her buddy, but there was no one waiting for her. Where was Dice? He was nowhere to be seen. He was hiding. He had sensed things were not right, and he knew his illness was taking its last tragic toll. I tend to think he hid in an attempt to protect the one person in his life he loved and cherished most. Finally, Kathleen found him, then caressed and tried to comfort him. He was so fragile and weak. Kathleen held him close on her lap and began preparing to take him to an emergency clinic. But before that could happen, Dice died right on her lap—the place where he felt most comfortable to let go in peace, with the person he loved the most. Kathleen carried him in her arms and headed to the clinic. Living in an apartment meant she would need help from the veterinary staff to make final decisions on handling his remains.

While the story of Kathleen and Dice beautifully illustrates the special kind of love that can be shared between owner and pet, it also teaches us that when we love, we will one day have to let go. When we don't expect it is time to let go, it hurts even more. After which, each of us will have to make the important EOL decisions on how to handle and manage the remains of our beloved companion—another difficult yet necessary task for us all.

The love between a person and a pet is simple. Pets live with you, love you, and are there for you every day. They are an integral part of your life and routine. They sense when you are hurting or don't feel well. When you're a mess or sweaty or have bad breath, they are still waiting for you, wanting to spend time with you. You could have a super tough day and, somehow, when you come home and see that sweet face looking up at you, that's all you need. It's the full definition of unconditional love, which can be something rare some people perhaps never quite truly experience with another person. Pets are incapable of harboring negative feelings toward someone they love.

You develop a special language where you can communicate with no words. All they have to do is give you a certain look, and you know what they're thinking. Likewise, you can furrow your brow and they instantly know they're in trouble.

Our pets depend on us. They can't exist without our care,

and that cements a very strong bond. When you sacrifice and serve another being, there's an indescribable connection. You learn from them, have fun with them, enjoy their companionship, and just want to be around them. There's nobody else who quite makes you feel the way they do, and it is simply unique unto itself.

The love you feel for a pet can shape who you are as a person. After seeing the way Wookie loved all of us, I've been able to look at my two-footed family through new eyes. She taught me so much about unconditional love, and that has helped me to really appreciate my human family in a whole new way. To love and be loved back is extremely poignant and powerful.

These factors make pet loss uniquely painful. It helps to remember this if feelings of confusion and guilt related to your grief begin to creep in.

CONFUSION

At some point in your grief journey, you might begin to wonder if there is something wrong with you. You might compare what you're feeling to a time when you lost a human loved one and realize you are much more upset now. It hurts differently inside, and it is hard to describe and explain, not only to yourself, but to others as well.

You might begin to think, "What's wrong with me? This is an animal. This is a pet. The other loss was a person. I shouldn't feel this way." The reality is loss of a pet comes with a special grief that can be extremely sharp and, in some cases, even more poignant than what accompanies human loss. This might not feel "right," but it is common and nothing to feel guilt or shame over.

If you live alone, you also might feel a heightened sense of loss. The loneliness you feel along with your grief can be debilitating, and it's not something to be taken lightly. If you don't have anyone to share your feelings with, the pain can be stronger. Having someone to talk to who knew your pet—a family member, friend, or neighbor—allows you to talk through the emotions.

If you don't have such options, talk with your vet. They have been through this process countless times and can help. Explain that what you're feeling is stronger and deeper than what you anticipated. They will respond with words of comfort and likely a recommendation for resources that can help.

WHY DOESN'T ANYONE UNDERSTAND?

Be reminded again that, when you lose a pet, you will inevitably encounter people who cannot remotely relate to what you're going through. People who have never been pet owners might respond unsympathetically to your pain by saying, "Don't be so upset. It was just a pet." Interestingly enough, I have spoken with other pet owners who have never experienced the loss of an animal as intensely as I have. They enjoyed and liked their pet, but expressed they were not really that close to them. They did not develop the unique and close-knit personal bond that I did with Wookie. The words they offer will leave you feeling as if there is no way they could possibly understand your situation—and they don't. Let's face it, they'll make you angry.

Though it might be hard to understand, those people aren't intentionally trying to hurt you. They simply cannot relate. It is not wrong to feel this way, and your feelings are completely valid as well. The perspectives in both situations are totally different and unique unto themselves, like two different sides to a coin. Don't let those kinds of comments tear down your spirit or make you feel like the love you have for your pet companion wasn't real.

It does not help that the level of grief pet owners feel after losing a pet is not externally validated in our culture. In many ways, society accepts grief over the loss of a family member or friend much more so than the loss of pets.

While places of employment often provide days off for the

loss of a family member, they rarely acknowledge the loss of a pet. However, I hope to see a shift here, as thinking around the topic evolves. In Europe, there are now some companies starting to give bereavement days for pet loss, and I applaud them.

HEALING IS A JOURNEY

Our feelings consume us when we don't take ownership of them. This first thing we have to do is allow ourselves to feel them. Granted, hurt and grief are emotions no one wants to feel, but healing cannot happen until we allow them in and work through them.

This might feel overwhelming at first, but by taking responsibility for your healing and allowing yourself the time and patience to complete the journey, you will improve. Make no mistake, it does take an inordinate amount of patience and time. You are the only person who can choose to mend yourself. Your life needs you to go on. There are things you need to do and people you need to take care of.

Ask yourself, "What can I do for myself today to make it better?" Sometimes, that means taking a walk or talking with a loved one. Sometimes, it means doing something new that doesn't remind us of our pet. Reaching out and helping others or volunteering can bring an extra boost of joy. By caring for others, we care for ourselves. When we lose ourselves in serving others, we find ourselves.

The one thing we can't do as we navigate all this is feel guilty for experiencing grief and pain at the loss of our pets. Pay attention to how you are responding to the loss, both emotionally and physically. You might experience body aches, headaches, or a number of other physical symptoms. Losing a loved one can take a huge toll and make you feel very tired. A good night's sleep can work wonders. If you need to and if possible, perhaps take a sick day. Consider talking with your physician. Take action to promote your own healing by being an advocate for your health and well-being.

MEN AND MOURNING

In my experience, men often mourn differently than women, in that they expect themselves to handle anything and everything, to be able to get over loss quickly and with little effect on their day-to-day lives. The degree to which they feel the pain is often surprising, both to themselves and to others around them.

This became apparent to me when I saw the intense impact losing Wookie took on both Randy and Will. They were totally devastated, and it showed. Losing a pet is always difficult for everyone, and there is never a good time for it to happen. This is why everybody needs someone to show extra compassion and caring and be there to love, support, and soften their broken heart at this harrowing time.

Several months ago, I had spent some time with my friend and business associate, Tucker. I shared my own pet loss story, and he told me all about his special buddy and companion, Murph. Just listening to him talk, I knew how much she had meant to him. She had captured his heart, and the two shared a wonderful bond for more than ten years.

Murph had endured a difficult bout with cancer and underwent medical treatment and procedures. Everything seemed to be going well for a few months, when Murph's health unexpectedly declined. The cancer had returned, and this time she was not able to fight it. Murph lost her battle to the disease at a time that could not have been worse for Tucker and his family. Tucker had just become a father with his first child, had just started a new business venture, and was already mourning the loss of a human friend. He barely had time to breathe, let alone grieve and go through the pain associated with the loss of his dog.

It was a devastating time and extremely stressful period in his life. After the pace slowed down somewhat, Tucker recalled: *It felt like an emotional meltdown. The grief was extremely overwhelming, even well after the fact.* For Tucker, it was a wonderful experience to welcome a new child into his life and exciting to begin the journey of developing a new business, but to compound those things with the loss of a friend and his beloved Murph was too much. The intensity of his grief took him by surprise, as it can with any of us.

We, as a society, both men and women, can be stereotyped, and sometimes there's a tendency to expect men to be stoic and strong. We generally don't often see them cry or show excessive emotion. But their hearts are just as fragile, completely capable of love and deprivation from loss. The bonds they develop with their pet companions run just as deep.

We must pay special attention to the men and women alike in our lives who might be affected by grief, and make sure they understand and share their emotions in the way they need to. We can encourage them to share their thoughts and feelings, and let them know it is okay to be sad. When we are there to support and console them, they in turn can be there to support us.

We can encourage everyone to share their thoughts and feelings. Grief is not a weakness. It is a sign of the love, devotion, and caring you possess within your heart. You must care for yourself, just as you take such great care of others.

Having Just Lost a Pet

THE FIRST DAYS AND WEEKS

We know we cannot have our pets forever, so we need to enjoy and cherish their special memory.
—BRITTANY GEORGE

The first days, even weeks, after losing your pet involve intense heartbreak and sorrow. You likely will find these days to be the most difficult, and as you move through them, you will feel a wide range of other emotions layered with your grief.

THE KÜBLER-ROSS MODEL

Just as many of us do in the wake of losing a human loved one, we will experience the Kübler-Ross model, also known as the five stages of grief, when coping with the death of a pet. You can expect to experience denial, anger, bargaining, depression, and, eventually, acceptance. Not being a medical professional, I share this grief-loss model, as it is widely used and often referenced as a professional tool. I share it for that purpose only.

You must take ownership of your grief, so you can move through all the steps and come out on the other side, recovered and whole. Think of it as watching television: you land on a channel and decide you don't like it, so you begin flipping through other channels randomly, trying to find something that feels more comfortable. Grief works much the same way. We need to be able to recognize when we can't stay somewhere and it's "time for a different channel."

Grief hinders emotional stability. The more we understand

how heartache and pain are part of the process, the easier it is to positively press forward.

DENIAL

When loss is new, it's tempting to deny the reality of the situation. We know in our minds that it's real, but our hearts can't believe or accept it. This is especially true when we're not expecting what has happened.

You might find yourself pretending, feeling the loss didn't happen. Such thinking is natural, although be careful not to become stuck in this stage. We must be willing to accept the loss to move on from the pain.

ANGER

When faced with situations out of our control, we feel helpless, and that can often lead to anger. This feeling can become particularly strong when we lose a pet to an accident, natural disaster, or complications related to a surgical procedure, or if they go missing or die young. We feel robbed of our time with them. We want more time and realize this is not going to happen.

If you begin to feel this way, there is no shame in releasing some of the anger in a way that's not harmful to anyone else. Cry, cry, cry, and then cry some more. Let it all out. Get the emotion out to rid yourself of some of the frustration. It will help you acknowledge how upset you are and take ownership of it. Sometimes, you simply must let it all out.

None of this guarantees you won't be angry from that moment on, but it does create a turning point. You allow yourself to feel all those overwhelming emotions, and then you are able to get it together and face the situation head on.

BARGAINING

In the bargaining phase, you might begin to question how things would or might have been different had you handled them differently. The word "if" becomes your enemy. You torture yourself thinking about ways you might try to change the situation. Just take the word "if" totally out of the equation. Do not use it at all. Bargaining becomes particularly powerful when euthanasia was the ultimate decision.

The painful answer is there is no way to change what's happened, especially when an EOL decision was made euthanizing your pet companion. You must remind yourself, as often as you need to, that you did what you did because you wanted what was best for the animal. You made the best decision you could. You put their QOL first, and that is what matters most for everyone involved, including you.

We put so much weight on our shoulders when we make decisions for our pet companions. Remind yourself that you made a choice to keep your pet from continuing to suffer.

DEPRESSION

Living with a broken heart can change us in ways we never imagined. We hurt in ways we never did before. You might feel broken and shattered beyond repair, and this horrific feeling might seem like it will never go away.

Recovering from the depression that comes with grief can take time, but it's necessary to the healing process. You must allow yourself to cry. It is therapeutic. Think of it as a tank that has too much pressure - you must let some of that pressure out or the tank will explode.

Sometimes, we need something soothing to hold onto as we allow ourselves to grieve through tears. After I lost Wookie, I would pick up something soft, such as a teddy bear, and close my eyes and cuddle it. I knew Wookie wasn't there, but it helped me to imagine her in my arms for just a few moments. I could caress something soothing and evoke special memories of her. Taking a minute to cuddle something soft was calming. That is exactly what I needed at the moment. Remember to take time to embrace a loved one. Hugs are healing to a broken heart.

Do whatever you need to do to comfort yourself, and don't feel funny about it, especially if it helps you release some of the sadness you've been holding back. With enough time, you will begin to realize you will not always feel this way.

ACCEPTANCE

Once the depression begins to subside, you will find yourself moving toward acceptance. At this point, you will be able to acknowledge the fact your pet is gone, and that isn't going to change. You might still feel sad, but you are able to put the pain in its proper place so you can begin to adjust to the new normal of your life.

The loss will no longer feel fresh, but that won't stop memories from flooding your mind and heart from time to time. You might still experience days when you wake up and think, "Time to take the dog outside," as I did for many weeks after Wookie's death. Experiencing those little blips are part of life and loss, and eventually they might just fill you with joy at the memory of your loved one. One day, you might even laugh at yourself in the process. You will realize even more fully that it is all normal. Life happens every day, come what may; there is no stopping it. Joy is always there, sometimes temporarily hidden behind a cloud.

RELAPSES AND DELAYED REACTIONS

Do not be surprised if one day you seem to be feeling fine then suddenly, totally unexpectedly, you feel your spirits sinking. Relapses are normal, but it's important not to let them undo the progress you've made. You must expect them to happen, sometimes at the most inopportune moments.

The best way to get past them is to get outside yourself and do something positive. By redirecting your emotions toward something positive, you can keep functioning and not let the pain drag you down.

You also might experience a delayed reaction. You might return to work shortly after the loss and feel seemingly fine, then, one day, you can't seem to focus properly or get motivated to do anything. This is your grief, and it will demand your attention in any way it can. No matter how much you hurt, you have to keep living your life. You have to care about yourself and your family, whether that involves other pets, spouses, children, parents, or anyone else you're responsible for. It is just as important that you tend to your own needs, as you cannot take care of anyone else if you're not taking care of yourself.

HELP THROUGH THE MOURNING

There are a variety of ways you can help yourself heal as

you move through your grief. As discussed in chapter 5, a memorial service can be a healthy way to begin to find closure, and there are several other approaches to take in your daily life that will continue to lead you on the path to recovery.

STAY ACTIVE, EAT RIGHT

Engaging in physical activity is a great way to stay healthy both physically and emotionally during your mourning period. It is very important to make and take time to exercise, go for walks, ride your bike, reflect on all that's going on, and focus on positive things in your life. Do something fun and uplifting, call a friend, or take your spouse or children out for some dedicated getaway time, even if only for a day or afternoon. Take time to reflect on how lucky you were to have your pet in your life and the joy you experienced. Move and get motivated to push yourself positively forward. A change of environment is a good opportunity to recharge your happiness battery.

Use this time to give yourself a pep talk, and encourage yourself to stay positive and celebrate your pet's life. Celebrate the fact that you are alive and that life is good: it's real even when the going gets tough. Remember to enjoy and talk and walk with friends and family. Laugh and smile with those you love. Enjoying the fresh air and sunshine really does a world of good. The sunshine is brighter outside.

Go visit a local museum or gallery. Find beauty in art and nature; it abounds and surrounds us, so take it all in and enjoy it.

If you are single or live alone, reach out to friends and family. It might be tempting to isolate yourself, but we are all stronger together. Interaction with others is key to recovery.

Nourishing your body with good-for-you foods is another easy way to stay energized and upbeat. Food plays an important role in our overall well-being. Make sure you are getting proper rest and plenty of sleep at night to give your body the strength you need to heal.

TAKE TIME OFF

As previously discussed, there is no harm in taking some time off from work if you have the ability to do so. Even a day or two can give you a positive mental boost and the time you need to rest and just breathe.

If you're really struggling with letting go, and your emotions are keeping you trapped in the anger or depression stages, you could possibly be at risk for physical illness. In this instance, you need to take care of yourself and give yourself a couple of sick days, if you can.

DIVERSION

Sometimes, you will simply need to find ways to distract yourself from the feelings of sadness and hurt. Figure out what makes you happy and take time to make it happen.

Maybe you enjoy serving others or volunteering. Visit an elderly neighbor. Bake some cookies or take some flowers over to brighten their day. Play with your kids or have a movie night.

Just because we are hurting does not mean we must stop doing the things we love. Whatever that is for you, carve out time and do it. It will remind your heart of all the joyful things left in your life.

REACH OUT, RECHARGE, REFRESH FROM WITHIN

If talking through your pain is helpful to you, try to do so with someone who knew your pet or who also has experienced the loss of a pet, or with a friend who loves you unconditionally and is willing to listen. They can share stories with you and sympathize in ways others might not be able to. Everyone loves to talk and share memories of pets they have loved and lost. You share your stories, and they can share theirs. It's a win-win for everyone.

Three days after I lost Wookie, I met with my book discussion group in my home. Wookie became a major topic of discussion. My friends were concerned about me and my well-being. Each had unique experiences with their own pets. We all shared touching stories, and ended up really helping and supporting each other. It almost felt like a grief support group. It was so good for me to know my friends understood and really felt what I was feeling. Knowing I wasn't alone helped me begin to heal.

It is not healthy to suppress your grief. When you suppress pain, it grows deeper. We've all heard stories of people who push their grief and anger deep down inside and never let it out. They grow bitter, living in a state of constant misery. Don't let yourself get to this point.

As time progresses, if you feel you're not moving positively forward or feel you need even more help, talk to your vet or primary care doctor about grief-counseling groups, or speak with a church minister or other religious leader if you are close to one. The idea of counseling might make you uncomfortable, but it can be the necessary step that keeps you from falling into depression. You need to be around others who understand what you're going through.

Remember, someday you might be the one someone turns to for support. This experience will help you guide that person during the time of their own pain.

CHARITABLE WORK

Charitable work can have a profound impact on both those we serve and ourselves. When you're compassionate toward others, whether it's people or animals, positivity grows inside you. It gives you the chance to forget what you're going through and think about others.

Lending a helping hand graciously can be so therapeutic. There are many ways to do so. Perhaps consider volunteering at an animal rescue shelter, if you feel up to it. Local food banks are always in need of help. When you lose yourself serving others, you find yourself.

While none of these activities offers a path to pain-free days or a chance to skip the grieving process entirely, they can offer you a break and positive reprieve from the pain and heartache. There is nothing wrong with finding a moment to relax your mind and heart, so you can have the strength for the rest of the journey ahead.

Handle with Care

YOUR CHILDREN—AND OTHER PETS IN YOUR HOME

The battles that count aren't the ones for gold medals. The struggles within yourself—the invisible, inevitable battles inside all of us—that's where it's at.
—JESSE OWENS

Whatever hurt and sorrow you are feeling, you can be sure your children's feelings are magnified. Their understanding of the situation will be different from yours. For most children, losing a pet could be their first experience with death and the associated grief. Every child will handle loss differently. You must prepare yourself to support them emotionally.

Children need your guidance and support just as much as you need the support of others. If this is their first encounter with loss, they need you to be their strength. Though this may not be easy to do as you navigate your own pain, being strong for them will ultimately aid your own recovery.

While their understanding of death might be limited, children can sense the strong intensity of the change. This goes beyond recognizing the pet is gone from the home. The shift extends beyond the lack of their physical presence. After Wookie passed away, the first time my kids and grandkids came into the house, their reaction to this shift was noticeable. They knew it. I could tell just by their body language and the way they spoke that they sensed the difference, despite not spending every day in the home with Wookie.

As you consider how you can be there for your children, remember the most important thing you can do to best serve others is to care for yourself. You must make sure you are tending to your own needs so you can be strong for those who might require extra care and attention during this difficult time.

Situations like these are opportunities for parents and grandparents to teach kids about how blessed we are to have our pets. It is a time to explain that, while pets come into our homes and family, we never know how long we will have them, and the time might be very short. Therefore, we need to love and treasure them while we can and hold memories of them close in our hearts.

It's also an opportunity to teach children how to grieve. They will watch as their parents go through the sorrow that comes with losing someone they love. When they see the tears and heartache, it teaches them it's okay to hurt and cry, and they learn how to release some of that grief. It validates their pain. Rather than disguising emotions, the parents are showing their children how to deal with loss and move positively forward with life. But excessive grief and tears might overwhelm them. We need to be careful and think of their needs.

BEING THERE FOR KIDS

As is the case with most circumstances in life, the most important thing you can do for your kids when they are grieving is love them. Go out of your way to be kind. Give them special hugs and hold the younger ones on your lap. If you notice angry or aggressive behavior, be patient and surround them with love. Don't give in to the temptation to be angry: be kind, patient, and affectionate in return when they're moody or grumpy. Love is a much more soothing medicine.

Each time you feel yourself hurting, remember your children are hurting, too. Pull the family together and talk about the reality of what's happening and what everyone is going through. You might recognize it's time to put aside your own grief and help them heal. Focus on and serve them. As you serve others, you serve yourself and allow yourself to grow. You're touching the lives of others who need you.

When you remove the focus from yourself and put it on others, you begin to truly give the gift of love to someone else. This is where healing happens. If we're focusing on ourselves and not pulling out of what we're dealing with internally, there's no room for reaching out to others. We are diminishing our capacity to love and serve. In order to grow, learn, and experience positive change within ourselves, we have to extend outward. By showing compassion to others, our hearts expand and begin to mend.

When one of our daughters was going through some growing pains, she spoke with Randy about her struggles. His advice was simple: go do something good. "Serve someone else," he said, "and I bet you'll realize the things you're going through aren't so tough. There are others whose situation is much worse." She decided to work at a food bank. This became a routine for her. Any time she started to struggle or become too focused on her own problems, she would say, "I better get out and do something to help somebody."

She realized how much that helped her. We taught her that when you stop focusing on yourself and help others, you will feel better every time.

Other times, it helps to have other outlets and diversions to help soothe a child's pain. There are many movies for younger children that tell stories of families losing their pets or loved ones. Many years ago, our young family was touched by the movie *All Dogs Go to Heaven*. What movies, if any, parents choose to show their kids is completely based on their own comfort level, but, a lot of times, movies can help reach children at their level to help them understand loss. They can soften the rough edges of their broken hearts and enable them to smile or grin, perhaps even laugh a little. Some talk about or reference pets going to heaven and rainbow bridges, while others focus more on the love shared between the family and the pet. This also can create a teaching opportunity, when you have a family movie night and take time to talk with the kids about the content before and after. Take a family walk, play a game, picnic in a park, go to the museum, or engage in some other fun, uplifting activity.

Finally, as mentioned previously, a memorial service is a good way to help children feel a sense of closure. It provides a time for kids to say goodbye to their pets. They are able to release some grief and begin to feel a little more prepared to move forward from their pain. Through all of this, you are instilling them with positive life skills.

HONESTY IN LOSS

How honest you should be with your kids is directly linked to the very role you play in their lives. You are their care-taker and advocate. They look up to you as an example and watch to see how you handle different situations in life. You are their primary role model. Who better than you to help them learn how to deal with grief and loss?

Do not lie to your children or try to hide your feelings from them. Honesty mixed with heartfelt compassion is the best policy. It's okay to let them see your heart is broken. It can be a lesson in compassion. They might say, "Gee, Mommy and Daddy feel bad, but they still love me and take care of me. They're trying to help me feel better, even though they hurt, too." A valuable lesson is taught.

When parents wallow in their own misery and fail to be there for their children, they are making a bad situation worse. The children are already missing their pet, and now they will have the added pain of feeling their parents aren't there for them. That can be devastating for a young child.

As painful as it may be, children need to learn they will lose those who are close to them. Grief presents an opportunity to teach them that, while every life comes with difficult situations, we have to press forward and find the positive. These life experiences give us a chance to teach about the heart, cherishing special memories, and the importance of caring for each other. By teaching them about the responsibility they have in grief—both to help themselves heal and to show kindness and compassion to others around them—we help them grow. It is therapeutic to everyone.

Be sure you speak to your children in a compassionate, tender manner that is age-appropriate. It will make all the difference in the world to let them know you care and are there to support and help them heal, whether they are two, twelve, or twenty years old.

Guiding children through loss can be a great teaching opportunity on the realities of life. Don't let these teaching moments pass. They are some of life's most important lessons. Who to be better taught by than mom or dad, or perhaps grandma or grandpa?

When people feel their kids can't handle a situation, they sometimes tell them lies with the intention of protecting them. Perhaps they say the pet has a new home and has gone to live on a wonderful farm where he has many friends to play with and plenty of room to run. This approach is a waste of an opportunity to teach children about the realities of life. It also ignores the fact the children will eventually find out the truth one day. When that times comes, what will they think of their parents? How will they react? Will that moment cause more pain or anger than they would have felt if they'd been told the truth?

All that being said, how you handle loss with your children is ultimately up to you. Take special care as you make decisions about how and what you will teach them. Love them and don't disguise the truth. Allow it to serve as a teachable moment for your family. You might be surprised at their capabilities and ability to bounce back.

LOSS AND OTHER FAMILY PETS

Oftentimes, people don't think about the effect loss has on other family pets. Multiple pets within a home also develop special, unique relationships. They have their own bonds. When one of them is suddenly gone, it changes the dynamic in the home. Their scent is still present, but that pet companion isn't physically there. Their toys and bedding disappear. The remaining pets know and sense there's been a change. Pets lose their pet companions and special pals, too. They are affected by the loss. They spent time together, often slept together, and created unique bonds. It's important to be aware of what your other pets may be going through and show them a little extra love and attention. Comfort them to show everything is okay.

There are a few red flags to look for when determining if your remaining pet is suffering from the loss. He or she might stop eating or become lethargic. They might whine and even search for their missing companion.

You also might notice a change in the hierarchy if multiple pets remain. If the animal that passed was the alpha, another pet might assume that role. The change in dynamics may cause confusion to the others, because they're used to reacting to the original alpha.

The pet might also watch you closely and react to any signs of distress you show. Pets can tell when people they love are unhappy, and it can be very confusing to them. Go out of your way to give them extra attention and care.

Recovering from Grief

THE FIRST YEAR

Optimism is the faith that leads to achievement.
—HELEN KELLER

The loss of a pet is devastating on many levels. A relationship you have spent a great deal of time nurturing and cherishing is gone. How can such trauma to your emotions be expected to vanish within a couple of days or weeks? That relationship was a part of your life, and it will take time to heal in its absence.

Do not despair if you are still hurting after several weeks or even months. You will not always feel this way, and there are several things you can do to help the healing process along. But your life has changed. It will be different.

WHEN IT STILL HURTS

The most important thing you can do is take ownership of and responsibility for your recovery. As much as we'd like someone with a magic wand to wave away our problems, that is not going to happen. We must be positive and proactive in our own right and actions. You must look yourself in the mirror and recognize the responsibility is on your shoulders. Having a support system in place will help you continue to move forward on the road to healing, but you ultimately have to be strong and take ownership of your situation.

No matter your circumstances, you are going to get through this. While everyone is special, totally unique, and completely different, and the details of their story vary, there are a significant number of commonalities involved in the grieving process. In a way, there is a recipe for recovery—a list of things people can do to get themselves back on track and put the missing pieces of their broken hearts back together. Your life will be changed, but it will go on. Things will just be different.

Grief doesn't go away by pretending it doesn't exist or by

burying it deep down. There's no hole deep enough to make it disappear. Moving forward means taking responsibility. It means taking positive steps, caring for ourselves, getting rest, serving others, and being accountable for the things we need to do and for our families. As we take steps to do that, each and every day, the magic of time begins to heal us. You will not wake up one day with a perfectly healed heart wrapped in a beautiful bow. You must trust its ability to mend slowly over time.

If you find yourself struggling to move on, it might be time to really ask yourself, "Do I want to be miserable and continue feeling sad and unhappy?" In all likelihood, the answer is of course not. While there are those who choose to put on blinders and ignore their feelings of devastation, really now, who truly wants to stay miserable? People who choose to remain stuck allow the loss to change them in a negative way as the anger lingers. There are many ways to avoid letting this happen to you. An attitude of gratitude for the gift of memories your pet brought you is priceless.

You can start small: baby steps, putting one foot forward at a time. Write positive affirmations on a Post-it note each morning or give yourself a pep talk when you start to feel drained. Create a list of things you'd like to accomplish and look at it throughout your day to keep motivated. Make it a point to do the things that make you happy and bring light and laughter back. This is the time to be an advocate for yourself, engage with life, and work to make yourself better. Faith and prayer have worked wonders for many.

Some days will feel harder than others. You'll think, *I'm still feeling pretty rough. I'm really feeling horrible. What can I do to get past this?* On those days, put a little extra energy into thinking about all the good things in your life. Think about the blessings. Focus on the memories you have of your pet, and think about the joy they brought. Our memories are permanent fixtures in our hearts. They don't go away; they are there to draw on and enjoy. Reflect on all those moments when they helped you or gave you unconditional love, and when you showed them love in return. That's joy, and that's very powerful. Those moments are some of life's most precious gifts. When you take the time to let the joys and wonderful experiences outweigh the loss, you'll feel your heart begin to mend, and each day will bring hope.

HOW LONG WILL I GRIEVE?

When you're in the midst of struggling with loss, you may find yourself asking, *How long will I feel like this?* The answer to that question is different for each person. The way grief affects each life varies, depending on the relationship the pet owner had with the one they lost.

Sometimes, grief alters portions of ourselves forever. I have a friend, a lovely woman, who lost her husband. Together, they had served others in the community and were involved in many activities. But after he passed, she stopped going to activities where family was involved. She'd say, "That's something Joe and I did together. I can't do it by myself." As one of her friends, along with many others, I understand and see that as her way of dealing with her pain. We all realize that's her comfort zone. Yet, she leads a happy productive life, continues to faithfully serve others and be a part of her community, and she continues to be actively engaged with her family, friends, and church. The loss she experienced simply caused that portion of her heart to pull away from specific activities, not from life itself or living a good one.

While we can't avoid adapting to the changes loss brings to our lives, we can expect the pain of grief to eventually subside. The more you take responsibility and work at recovery, the better each day will become. You miss the one you've lost, but the more you engage with others in your life—those you love and serve—the better it will be.

ACCEPTING YOUR LOSS

The best way to begin to accept a loss is to understand what you're going through. Find out more about what you're feeling. Perhaps read more about the Kübler-Ross stages of grief and know what to expect (see chapter 7 for more information). Knowing more about what you're going through will help you face it head on and allow you to be realistic about your pain. You'll see that life will be different, but that there's light, love, and joy beyond the struggle.

The gift of our pets was never meant to last forever. We knew there would be a time we had to let go. Compared to human life, a pet's life is very short. We might have the opportunity to love several pets in our lifetime. This is a foundational truth you must be able to accept to appreciate the gift you had in that pet.

KEY INGREDIENTS OF ACCEPTANCE

The first ingredient in acceptance is time. No heart can mend without it, and healing will not happen overnight. Though you want the pain to go away immediately, it simply won't, and that is a fact.

The second ingredient is time's companion: patience. You need patience to recognize time is necessary for healing. You need to be patient with yourself as you heal. You will especially need patience for the bad days, and there will be many, particularly in the beginning. You must be patient with yourself for the times you think you are doing great, then suddenly something little sets you off—a sight, a smell, a sound—and drags you right back down. You also must be patient with other family members, friends, or acquaintances, especially when they cannot relate to what you are going through or feeling.

These moments can come out of nowhere. One day, long after Wookie's death, my husband and I were out for a walk and met a couple who were walking a pair of schnauzers. They were the same size and silver color as our Wookie. I looked at them, and suddenly, bam—the memory of Wookie hit me. These two pups looked so similar they could have been her brothers or sisters. I went over to pet them, and it was like petting Wookie. An ache swelled in my heart as the power of her memory overwhelmed me. Then I realized how good it felt to pet some cute dogs who reminded me of my sweet companion and the memories we shared. Suddenly, I changed my attitude, which elevated a more positive attitude of healing within.

These things will and are going to happen, and there's no way to prepare for or avoid them. You must be patient, allow yourself to feel them, and then let them pass. Change your focus to more positive things or thoughts. You might think: *It's been months! Why am I still feeing this way?* The answer is that you might always feel this way to a certain extent. But again, a broken heart longs to be mended. Think back to the wonderful philosophy of *kintsugi*. It is a powerful tool.

The smallest thing can remind you of your pet or loved one, and even make you act in ways you would never expect. One day, I was cleaning the laundry room and found a little kernel of Wookie's dog food. I couldn't imagine how I'd missed it. I held it in my hand, looked at it, and a wave of memories began to flood my mind. I couldn't bring myself to throw it away. It seems so silly now when I think about it, but it wasn't silly then. I set it on the counter. I wasn't ready to just toss it away, because it was Wookie's. But the next day, I was able to remind myself that everything was okay, and it was time to throw it away. I picked it up and let it go. I actually smiled and laughed at myself. Laughter is good medicine.

Patience is particularly important when you are also helping children cope with a loss. You must remember they also will experience relapses, just as you do. You might walk into the family room and find your little one sitting quietly near where their cat or dog once had their bed. They might not even know what they're feeling or be able to articulate it to you, but you can see it. Your little ones feel the loss, and they're missing their special buddy they loved so much. That's your opportunity to show compassion and understanding and help them through it. You can help them learn to be patient with themselves. Remember that when you help others, you become the primary beneficiary of joy.

THE INEVITABILITY OF DEATH

Coming to terms with the inevitability of death can lead to acceptance. It is a harsh reality of life that everyone dies: your family, your friends, your pet companions, and eventually even you. We have no choice but to accept this fact, painful and upsetting as it may be. But understanding that the day of your pet's death was going to come, and that your pet almost certainly was not going to outlive you, can be a step in the healing process. This can be difficult to contemplate, but it is a truth we must all face.

When Wookie turned fifteen years old, I began mentally preparing myself for the inevitable. I thought: *As much as she seems pretty spry, she's only got a couple years left, and I don't know how long for sure.* I knew I needed to enjoy her. I snuggled with her and did all I could to appreciate her. I made each moment with her count, so when the day eventually did come, I knew I had taken full advantage of my time with her. It was time to hug a puppy.

I've noticed my children looking at me in a similar way. They see my husband and me getting older, and they're getting older too. Everyone eventually realizes the certainty of death. But in many ways, death is just another one of the constant changes that come with being alive. Everything and everyone changes. Whether we are watching our children grow, or changing careers, or moving to a new city, or preparing for retirement, life never stands still. Nor is it meant to. Change brings special opportunities to grow and excel.

The cycle of life never stops, and you can't have life without death. It's the universal truth. But it does not mean we cannot enjoy what we have while we have it. Something as simple as eating your favorite pizza or watching your favorite movie can make you happy. On a deeper level, our hearts are capable of unimaginable joy. Joy and the heart are intertwined, and our pets are a part of that joy. When they are no longer with us, a piece of our joy is lost, and the heart has to mend. But the good news is that the heart can expand to make room for more love and joy. Pain does not mean the end of joy. Memories shared are precious mementos to cherish always.

REMEMBERING THE GOOD TIMES

The time we have with our pets is a blessing. We can honor that gift by focusing on the good times we had with them. At first, remembering them in this way might seem like a double-edged sword, as pain can accompany the memories, but in time, you will see the way they touched your heart is something you will never forget.

I like to think about Wookie and how glad I am that she was a part of my life. She had such a great ability to bring people together and make them happy. We have countless memories of our children connecting with her. She balanced our family when we faced tough times, and she was there in the good times. After our family's various surgeries and medical recoveries, Wookie spent countless hours consoling us, cuddling close, and soothing our pain. Smiling sweetly during those difficult moments and letting us know she cared, she was our constant companion and there every day for each of us. Wook always knew when we needed her. She moved when we moved and was our fuzzy family mascot: she was a blessing. It was such a surprise and sweet joy to have her as long as we did, and I am grateful every day for it, every single moment.

Caribbean Christmas Memories with Wookie, her 5 boys, Melinda and special buddy Bill.

Think about your pet and the way they touched your heart. Think about the things they taught you, and how that made you a better person. Laugh about the stories they gave you. I still tell the story of Wookie and the broken vase to my grandchildren, showing them the many cracks. Now, I make a point to take a teaching moment to share *kintsugi* with them. They think that is pretty cool! My son John still remembers that day very well. It is part of our treasury of memories. Sharing such stories and looking back at our pets' lives allows their goodness and joy to stay with us.

JOURNALING

Writing can be therapeutic and a helpful way to work

through what you are feeling. You might find more memories coming to mind than you realized you had.

I journaled about my own grief journey for a full year after we lost Wookie. I'd write about what I was going through, the feelings I experienced, and the process of my grieving and memories of Wookie.

Journaling kept me moving forward. It gave me something physical to do. It was a great release for my grief. There's something about putting a pen in hand or typing away on the computer. Things come out differently when I write. I wrote to let it all go and did not read over what I'd written in its entirety for a year. Now and then, I'd get the inkling to open those pages, reading a few here and there, but reading them brought back pain, and I was not fully emotionally ready then. I read all I had journaled on October 31, 2016, one year after we lost Wookie. Because I was writing exactly what I was feeling at that moment, the words were sometimes rough to get through. But once some time had passed, I was able to look back at them and see how far I'd come. I'm so glad I took the time to capture those feelings and preserve them. It made a big difference in helping me mend those broken pieces of my heart, and I recognized I was in a more peaceful state of recovery.

And as I mentioned previously, many pet owners write

poignant, heartfelt appreciation letters that they dedicate to their companions. Writing is a wonderful release.

WHERE TO START

Writing and journaling don't necessarily come easily to most people. Sometimes, you just have to sit down and start writing. For me, I started documenting everything about what happened: the unexpected circumstances when we came home, Wookie's seizures and not recognizing us, everything. Everything covered in this book thus far is in that journal, and quite a bit more. Everything just flowed from me when the pen was in my hand or I was typing on the computer.

When you're not sure what to write, simply describe what's in your heart. Don't worry about spelling or sentence structure. Just write what you feel.

When you first start writing, you may find you want to write frequently. I spent the first several months writing almost every day. You might only feel the urge to write occasionally, and that's fine, too. Do what feels right for you as you work through these emotions by putting word to page. If you like to write by hand, get yourself a beautiful notebook and keep it nearby for when a memory or musing hits. Fill it up at your own pace.

Once you're done writing, set it aside. Put it away and don't read it again until some time has passed. Even if you're still struggling with your grief, you'll be able to read it and say, "Yes, what happened was terrible and really hard. I still feel the loss, but I've really come a long way since then."

SCRAPBOOKING

If you're not one for journaling, think about doing a scrapbook or something that involves working with your hands. This is a great way to channel your grief into something positive that you and the rest of the family can enjoy forever.

You can buy pieces of scrapbook materials at the store and then put them together and add commentary and photos. There are companies that do digital scrapbooks or photobooks that allow you to write little notes with each picture. However you chose to do it, the time spent looking at and reflecting on photos will not be wasted. Perhaps consider organizing those special photos of your companion so you can have them readily available and easily accessible when you want them.

If you have children in your family, have them help. Engaging the kids in making the scrapbook helps them work through their grief as well. Small children can even draw pictures of their beloved pet pal to create special, personal works of art. Let them share their touching tales about their pet companions. As they share their stories, you can write them down and preserve them. Encourage them to talk as they work, sharing stories and their special feelings. Think of it as a way to document the pet's life, as well as your cherished memories with them.

MEMENTOS

Displaying mementos is another way to ease your pain, while also celebrating your pet's life. You can frame a selection of favorite photos or any other relevant item. Miller, my friend who lost her horse, cut a piece of his mane and framed it. Some people save a cutting of a pet's fur.

You can also set up special displays of your keepsakes. As previously mentioned, we put Wookie's collar next to a special ceramic schnauzer Christmas tree ornament. We also put her special elf outfit on a stuffed bear. My grandchildren love these things, as it is a pleasant and fun way to remember our special pet. See chapter 5 for more on mementos.

FAITH IN RECOVERY AND ACCEPTANCE

When faith is part of who you are, it can be a very powerful tool in your recovery journey. You can take comfort in your understanding of eternity, and use your faith to find hope and encouragement to move forward.

If it helps, talk to your church leader and let them know you're going through a hard time. Talk about the role of faith in grief with your family, and ask for strength as you pray with them each day. Seek out books, scripture, or motivational tools to help bring your faith into the healing process. Remind yourself that your pet companion is in a better place.

Even if you are not religiously oriented, there are many philosophies and practices related to life, the universe, and the experiences we go through that can help you along your grief journey. Draw upon whatever best speaks to your heart.

Remember the vase from this book's introduction? When I learned about the healing philosophy of *kintsugi*, it was like the lights coming on. As a quick refresher, *kintsugi* is an old Japanese art that treats the broken pieces of pottery as a part of history specific to that item. Instead of disguising the breakage, we draw attention to it to celebrate the item's unique past. When we think of our hearts in the same way, we can celebrate how our lost pets touched us and how they are part of our own history. Our hearts are more beautiful for having loved them.

WHEN DEPRESSION GETS TOO STRONG

There are times when you need to take a close look at how you're feeling. Are you so consumed by pain that you're having a tough time doing things that are part of your normal routine, such as taking care of yourself, your home, or family? Is the weight of your grief so intense you can't imagine going on? If you are feeling this way, you need to do something more to get help. You can't stay in this state. Part of taking ownership of your situation is seeking help when you need it, so you can move forward.

If your struggle is deep, if it's disrupting your life and self-care, perhaps it's time to talk to someone. Open a dialogue with your vet. They see this all the time, and they experience the grief that comes with the very situation you're in. They can be a good source of comfort and offer recommendations and referrals. They can talk to you about where to go for help.

When you're facing all the pressure and strain of grieving, you need the right information.

That relationship with your vet can be a solid resource for the information you need. Do all you can to develop that relationship early in your pet's life so you have the foundation of trust already in place. They can talk to you about pet loss therapy and group activities.

You also can talk with a friend, perhaps someone who has experienced the loss of a pet and can truly be there for you. They can talk with you about their journey and what they went through. Just talking through the pain you're feeling can relieve the heaviness weighing down your heart. It allows you to share memories and remember the joy your pet companion brought to your life. It gives you the opportunity to remember the good.

If none of this is working, it might be time to seek the help of a professional. A therapist can help you understand what you're feeling and give you the tools you need to move past the pain so you can begin to heal and feel whole again.

BROKEN HEARTS ARE MEANT TO MEND

As you come to the end of your first year of grief, you will likely realize you've been through more than you ever could have expected. You've grieved, you've accepted the loss, and you've grown. You are changed, but that is okay. There is still much to be grateful for and, remember, your pet would not want you to be sad forever.

Our pets are a gift, a special joy in our lives, while we have them. Remember the wonderful times you shared with them. Perhaps by this time you created a scrapbook or pulled together a photo book of them. Keep your hands busy bringing together something positive to help counteract those feelings of loss. Mend the broken pieces so you can heal your heart.

As tough as it is, you have to get through this. And you will. You're going to feel better and your smile is going to come back. This might be a dark chapter in your life, but you'll get through it. You are resilient. In time, you will smile again.

Draw on your friends and family. Remember, most importantly, you do not have to bear everything alone. Allow others to be there for you, and make sure you take time to be there for others—especially the young children in your family. Get out and serve others, whether it be in your church, community, or family. Expand your horizon and your vision beyond yourself and your pain. You'll be able to draw in the sunshine after a storm.

The more you understand your grief, the better you'll be able to work through it and heal your heart. It takes time and patience. Be patient with yourself and realize that one day you'll have a great day and feel you have a handle on things, but the simplest thing may set you back. That's normal. It's going to happen. But the next day you'll start again.

It will get better. With time comes healing. Envision that

you're going to recover, and you'll get there. New beginnings come each and every day.

Helping Others, Sharing Love, and Compassion in Action

There is no pain so great as the memory of joy in present grief.
—AESCHYLUS

Now that you have lived through one of life's great challenges, you are equipped to help others do the same. When someone you know loses a pet, it becomes an opportunity for you to give back. The compassion and love you show those who are experiencing loss will be just as important to them as it was to you.

There are a number of ways to show you care. Some people send cards or framed photos. Sometimes, it's as simple as putting your arm around someone who needs some comfort. These little gestures make a big difference for someone who is hurting. Think about the things that helped you in your own recovery, and do the same for others.

SYMPATHY AND EMPATHY

When attempting to help someone who is in pain, it is important to know the difference between sympathy and empathy.

Sympathy is a feeling of concern or sorrow for someone who is experiencing a hardship. If you've lost a pet and you try to talk with someone about your feelings, but that person has never experienced the loss of a pet, they can sympathize with you. They can feel bad for you and say something such as, "Oh, wow, that's got to be difficult. I'm so sorry. I know that must hurt you." Their heart aches for you, but they are not able to fully put themselves in your shoes.

Empathy, on the other hand, is a little bit different. Empathy is the deep concern for someone and what they're going through, because you can fully understand what they are feeling. You might have gone through and experienced something similar personally, and you know the pain and grief. There's a direct tie to the heart because those people completely understand the overwhelming heartache: they've been there and felt the agony of that experience.

Compassion is sympathy or empathy in action. When we show compassion, we do something to counteract the pain someone else is feeling. It's opening your heart to promote healing in someone else's life.

HOW COMPASSION TOUCHED ME

When we lost Wookie, our vet became a great source of compassion for us. When I picked up Wookie's ashes, she asked me, "How are you doing? What's going on?" I was honest. I told her, "I'm totally miserable. This is one of the hardest things I've ever been through." So, we talked. She took the time to listen to what I was feeling. Her boarding tech Brittany was the gal who sent us the framed photo of Wookie along with a card, and I was sure to let our vet know about how greatly that act was appreciated. She showed me how much she truly cared by making time to talk with me.

Many of my friends also acted as great examples of compassion in action. A friend, Kelli, who loves to paint watercolors, typically of landscapes, graciously agreed to create a portrait of Wookie. I sent her some of my favorite pictures and she was able to truly capture her adventurous, free spirit on the canvas. She even framed it and told me the act of painting Wookie made her feel closer to my beloved pet. She would not accept any payment. What a generous gift. Her kindness meant so much. She'd shared her time and talents, and the painting has brought me endless joy.

Another buddy, Charis, dropped over one day and, to my surprise, handed me a sweet mini-quilt coaster that she had sewn and embroidered with the quote, *"Dogs leave paw prints on your heart"*. This was another example of compassion in action, but this time it was shown in a different way. Charis has never experienced the pain of losing a pet companion, but loves me and simply wanted to show she cared nonetheless. She wanted to do something that helped me feel better after losing Wookie, simply because of our friendship.

Charis was also the one who introduced me to *kintsugi*; she made me a magnet picturing a blue bowl mended with gold glue and shared the story of the art and philosophy. This is the poem written on the magnet, the last line is adapted from Isaiah 49:16:

The Savior of the world desires to mend
Our broken pieces, to fill our empty spaces,
To make of us a vessel that is
more beautiful and whole,
He does not hide His scars…
He has engraved us in the palms of His Hands.

—UNKNOWN

Again, if you are not religiously oriented, this poem still can touch broken hearts. There are countless other examples of compassionate and caring acts I could give, and each one proves you never run out of opportunities to show you care.

GIVE IT TIME

When attempting to help someone who is going through a difficult time, remember everyone grieves differently and goes through different phases as they do. They may not want to reach out or talk initially, and may need time alone or with their family. Soon after they first experience loss, they may not be at a point where they're emotionally ready to accept an act of kindness, much less discuss their loss.

This does not mean you've done anything wrong. It's important to take that leap and reach out, nonetheless, so they know you are there whenever they are ready. Do the best you can and keep trying, while respecting their space. You never know when they might need a friendly gesture most.

OTHER WAYS TO HELP

Sometimes, a person experiencing loss needs someone to advocate for them. Show them you take their pain seriously and will help them get the care they need, no matter what it entails.

Remember the many people who were quick to brush you off when you lost your pet—the ones who said things like, "It was only a pet." Do the opposite for those you care for. Validate their pain by listening and, when appropriate, sharing stories about your own grief journey. You are someone who is truly able to empathize, and in a way, that is a gift. Share that gift with the people in your life who are hurting.

Don't always wait for your loved one or friend to reach out and get back to you. Be proactive and check in with them from time to time, especially in the early days and weeks after their loss. As you well remember, those early days are often the hardest. Being there can be as simple as making a phone call or stopping by to say, "How's it going?" You may even consider making them a meal. When you deliver it, say, "Hey, I was thinking about you. I had this food and

I know it's tough right now. One less thing to worry about, so I made this meal for you." It's nothing huge, but it makes a difference for someone who's hurting. Sometimes all people need is the simple things. They may not be ready for more just yet, and that's okay. Small and simple heartfelt gestures provide big benefits on the receiving end.

If your loved one opts to hold a memorial service or other ceremony, be there. Just by showing a willingness to participate, you are validating their feelings. The most precious thing you can give someone is your time, and by setting aside a few hours to be there, you are showing them how much you care.

The most important thing you can do is act. Just saying you want to help or telling someone to let you know if they need anything is not enough. Do something. Whether it's sending a card or letter, taking your friend out to lunch, bringing a small gift for the kids, or any other act of kindness, the gesture will be appreciated. These things matter.

COMPASSION FATIGUE

Once again, please remember the people you have trusted to care for your pet will also be deeply affected by the loss of your animal and other animals their clients lose. They form attachments to the many pets they assist, including yours, and their grief should also be acknowledged.

Professionals who deal with loss on a regular basis often experience compassion fatigue. Compassion fatigue is stress and tension caused by excessive exposure to the suffering of others, and it is common in veterinary offices.

Vets are responsible for the act of physically administering the medications that send our pets to their final rest. While most enter into the profession knowing fully this will be part of the work, it remains a difficult task to perform.

Dr. Kim Eaton once told me, "We know every time we do that it's going to be hard. We have to do it, and we feel compassion. We especially feel compassion for the pet owner, yet we have to be able to cope within ourselves."

This is an immense burden, and one that can have a deep impact on any professional. When you consider the frequency with which they must perform such an act, the possible effects of such stress are daunting.

Compassion fatigue is not limited to vets. It can affect techs, boarders, groomers, foster animal caregivers, and anyone else who interacts regularly with pets and their families. They must not only deal with the loss of the animal; they'll want to try to console you as well. Being there emotionally for so many other people can be stressful. When times get tough, they shoulder a heavy burden. Our appreciation and acknowledgement are well deserved.

Compassion fatigue is a serious part of working with animals, especially for professionals in the industry. Sometimes they reach a point where, though they love their work, the emotional trauma becomes overwhelming. They are constantly dealing with loss. For some, the only choice is to leave the profession to maintain mental stability. We need to remember that our loss is their loss too.

COUNTERACTING WITH POSITIVITY

Many times, the best way to counteract compassion fatigue is to encourage the staff to open up about the reality of their emotions. They need to know that what they're going through is real and valid.

Let them talk and counsel them. Help them deal with what they're going through, so they can effectively do their jobs. There has to be a balance between feeling compassion for their client, feeling bad about the patient, and being able to protect their emotions in the process.

I have found the book *When Helping Hurts: Compassion Fatigue in the Veterinary Profession* by Kathleen Ayl to be a wealth of information on the topic. It addresses the importance of self-care, ways to help clients while protecting your own emotions, and how to find a compassion-fatigue specialist. It describes compassion fatigue as what happens when a caregiver who works continuously with the suffering of others stops taking care of his own needs. It stresses the importance of paying close attention to the signs of compassion fatigue and practicing self-care to avoid them.

As the Dalai Lama said:

> *Self-compassion is the first step*
> *toward compassion for others.*

In the midst of our loss, as we show compassion for others and ourselves, we need to realize that not everything is obvious. We won't always see how the loss of our own pet affects others. We need to reach out and help others, especially the caregivers who were a part of our pet's life.

One way to do so is to encourage them to read this book in hopes it will help them understand how the feelings of loss they experience are real, too. Their care for our pets is invaluable. They are appreciated more than they know, and we need to show them we care.

Getting a New Pet

*Until one has loved an animal, a part of
one's soul remains unawakened.*
—ANATOLE FRANCE

The right time to get a new pet will be different for every family. For some, it can be therapeutic and positive to quickly welcome a new pet into their home. With others, it has the opposite effect. And for some people, it might never happen. There should be no guilt in choosing not to get another pet; likewise, you shouldn't feel bad about bringing a new pet into the family. Everyone is different, with special needs, concerns, and circumstances. There is no one right answer for everyone.

This is a decision only you can make: you shouldn't allow the influence of others to impact your choice. This can be challenging, especially when children are involved. At some point, perhaps even when they are still grieving, they will likely ask, "When are we going to get another dog or cat?" They might be trying to fill that hole in their hearts and hoping a new pet will replace what they've lost. This could be a little red flag for parents. It can be an indication you need to be there a little more for that child, and they need to talk more about their struggle with you.

TIME TO HEAL

As is the case with so many aspects of grief, time is crucial. You must give yourself time before jumping into a decision about bringing home a new animal companion. In the early days of your grief, you might convince yourself that you just miss having a pet, when, in fact, you miss the specific little guy or gal you just lost. This can be especially true for children. It's okay for parents to decide the family needs more time to heal.

Attempting to "replace" your pet with a new one is not necessarily the best way to recover from grief. Often, it is a form of avoidance. Bringing a new pet into a home that is still grieving can complicate the situation. There might be expectations on that new pet to be like the old one, which is unfair and unrealistic. Placing such an expectation on a new pet can bring on feelings of resentment when things don't work out the way you'd hoped.

I have spoken with a number of people who admitted they adopted a new pet family member too soon. Most wished they had waited longer and taken more time to grieve for the pet they had lost. I have also spoken with people who said bringing home their new companion within a short grieving period was not an issue, and it was a very positive experience. In the end, it is a deeply personal decision with pros and cons on both sides.

You also have to consider the commitment bringing home a new pet requires. If you lost an older animal, then turn around and adopt a puppy, you will have a lot more work to do than you did previously. You'll have to house-train them, get them up-to-date on shots, and get them into a routine. They will fit into your lives in a different way than the pet you lost.

If you're not emotionally over the loss of your pet, all of this can overwhelm you very easily. You might even unintentionally cause a traumatic situation for you and your family. If more time is needed to figure this all out, take it.

Thinking about all this brings to mind Hamlet's well-known

soliloquy, in which he asked, "To be or not to be—that is the question." Only in this case it's, "To be or not to be pet owners again—that is the question." It also makes me think of the story of Snickers and Bella.

My friend LaMilla and her husband Don found Snickers at a small dog rescue facility. They had specifically requested an older animal and met Snickers when she was around age six.

They adopted her, welcomed her into their family, and went on to share life together for an amazing twelve years. She was their constant companion, awesome buddy, and the total joy of their lives. Of course, they were totally devastated to lose her.

Losing their sweet Snickers completely broke their hearts, and they made the decision not to bring a new pet into their home. But, as I always say, never say never. After six years, they knew their hearts were mended, and they could now embrace another pet family member. They went back to the small animal shelter, again requested an older animal, and found their precious little pooch, Bella, who was estimated to be around seven years old. Bella has been the light of their lives. She is as gentle-natured and beautiful as the name she bears.

There is a reason both Snickers and Bella were such good

fits for LaMilla and Don. Both times, they were smart in their approach to getting a new pet. They considered all factors and made a decision about what was best for them. An older dog with less energy, who was somewhat trained, made more sense for them. They got animals with calmer temperaments and decreased energy levels, and two older dogs that might not have been adopted otherwise got a loving home. It was a win-win for everyone.

To make your own experience a success, I encourage you to consider the following suggestions.

THE DOS AND DON'TS OF GETTING A NEW PET

If you do opt to get a pet after a loss, there are some important things to consider to make sure you're making the best decision for both yourself and the new pet family member, and that the timing is good for everyone involved.

THE DOS

Do make sure you're really ready to have a new pet in your home. Ask yourself whether you are confident your heart has fully mended from the loss you've experienced and healed from the grief. Make this a careful, thoughtful decision.

If you do bring a new pet home, view it as an opportunity

to establish a brand-new relationship. Welcome the new pet into your life as the unique individual it is, just as you would a new friend or family member.

This is also an opportunity to reestablish your relationship with your vet. This is a relationship you will want to nurture and cultivate for the duration of your new pet's life. Through the vaccinations, the well care, and the times they're sick, you're going to be depending on your vet to give you important information.

Consider calling your vet before you decide on a new pet to ask for their recommendations. The vet can talk to you about different breeds and which ones might be a good match for your family, and offer other helpful suggestions for you to consider.

THE DON'TS

Don't be impulsive. You might be tempted to use a new animal to quickly patch up the hole in your heart, but this can lead to disastrous results in the long run. I have seen this happen with several of my own friends and acquaintances. You have to be ready, emotionally, mentally, and physically, to bring a new pet home. You can't get there overnight. Bringing a new pet home simply because you're used to having one around is not the answer, either.

Don't get a new pet just because it's cute. This is easier said than done, especially when your grief is telling you to use that adorable little fuzzball as a Band-Aid, but don't give in. Also, don't let someone else convince you to do it because it will "cheer you up." Again, a quick fix is not the answer.

Do not expect your new pet to be just like the pet you lost. To reiterate: a new pet cannot be a "replacement." Animals are as unique as people. Don't give the new pet the same name as your old pet: talk about putting unrealistic expectations on the animal. This can be confusing emotionally for you and really unfair to your pet. Your new pet will have a different personality and quirks. You want to invite them into your family without expectations that are very likely to leave you disappointed. Allow your family to develop a unique relationship with this new member.

There are many pets and breeds. It is a lot to consider.

KNOW MORE BEFORE YOU DECIDE

There is a vast amount of information available about the different types and breeds of animals. Each has a different personality, temperament, needs, physical characteristics, and energy level. Doing some research on which one is a good fit for you will help you make the best decision.

The following are some factors to consider when choosing a new pet:

Needs

An animal's needs can include everything from grooming to health, and many other things in between. Some pets need to be trimmed and groomed regularly. Some animals are more susceptible to colds, digestive problems, or joint trouble. Some pets need to be extensively exercised regularly or have extremely high energy levels. Do you personally have the time, stamina, and energy to devote to such a pet? What about in the future? How will your energy and health be then? Some pets flourish more with the companionship of other animals. Consider everything you are willing and able to comfortably provide for the pet before deciding which one to bring home.

Lifespans

Think also about the fact that different breeds have different lifespans. If the animal you are considering typically lives a long life, are you willing to commit to its care for that duration of time? If the animal's lifespan is short, are you willing to possibly experience loss and grief again in only a few years?

HOME ENVIRONMENT

Think about any changes that have happened to your physical environment since you brought your last pet home. Did you live in an apartment before and now you're in a house, or vice versa? Is your home suited to a new pet? Will your home accommodate a large or small animal better? Did you have children in the home before who are now grown and out of the house?

If you rent, does your landlord allow pets, and are there guidelines on size, breed, or weight? Will they expect an additional monthly fee?

Also consider climate. Dogs with extremely heavy hair can be better suited for colder climates, while short-haired dogs might do better in warmer climates. Of course, in the day of air conditioning and climate control, this has become a more muted consideration than in the past. Cats are entirely a whole world unto themselves, with special needs and considerations.

PERSONAL SITUATION

Think about yourself and your ability to meet all the animal's needs. Consider your age, physical limitations, if any, and your ability to exercise a dog. Consider your work situation. Are you home often, or do you spend the bulk of your time at the office or traveling? Think about the future and where you'll be in five years: Does a new pet fit into that plan? If you are retired, does this change your considerations?

My husband and I have not adopted a new pet into our family since we lost Wookie. We never say never and know that time will tell. Our current decision has nothing to do with our love of having a family pet and companion in our home. I miss having a dog buddy around. My heart has healed and mended from the loss of our sweet Wookie. Do I ever still miss her? Of course. She was an amazing part of my life for a very long time, and I will cherish her memories always.

But our life has quickly evolved in many new, diverse, and unexpected ways since we lost Wookie. We spend a lot of time with our children and grandchildren. Life has become extremely busy, and we are positively engaged. Things are very different than when we adopted Wookie into our family in West Texas in 1999. Life changes every single day, often without us noticing it. Change quietly just creeps in.

Even without a full-time live-in animal companion in our home, I embrace spending time with animals, especially our children's and friends' pets. I love them all, just the way our children loved Wookie. They are all an important part of my life.

Aaron and Taylor's pooch, our grand-puppy Happy, is a tender-hearted sweetie you just cannot help but love. She is in complete doggie heaven snuggling close or sitting beside you. Happy is exactly what her name states: she is indeed happy and contented. She is a big shepherd mix who loves going on family walks and being exercised. We always enjoy spending time with this special grand-puppy of ours.

Happy loves her bed as a bed—and as a pillow.

When we visit Stephanie and Dale's crew, we are blessed to be surrounded by their two pooches. Angel and Duchess are very small, around nine pounds each. Angel is more than thirteen and slowing down a bit with age, but that does not slow down her love of life, family, and playing, or being a sweet cuddling companion. Duchess, the younger dog, is the friskier of the two, and she also adores her family and full-time companion Angel. I simply love the girls.

Angel and Duchess, "The girls", are precious beyond measure.

As I previously mentioned, we also have Lady Rambo, our feline family member, Lisa's cat and our grand-kitty. Lady is Lisa's special buddy of more than thirteen years. Lady adores Lisa, and Lisa adores Lady enough to let her hog her pillow at night when they cuddle and sleep beside each other. I have discovered the world of cats and their companions is similar in heart to that of dog owners. With my exposure to feline friends, I have come to appreciate and enjoy their unique personalities and the ways they show their affection to you. Many years ago, when a kitty first gave me a kiss, I about fell over, being someone who had only been familiar with dog smooches prior to that. I had no idea cats had rough tongues to clean and groom their fur. Lady has at times been glad to see me and given me a few sweet scratchy licks and leg caresses, but typically she is more of a one-person cat. She is totally devoted to her Lisa. It is so touching to see the way they are so bonded to each other.

We had an opportunity to care for our son Chris's giant schnauzer, Princess Leia, for a month. She is one year old, weighs over sixty pounds, and is totally in puppy mode. Her energy level is off the charts compared to our Wookie's simple, relaxed mode. Leia requires tons of run, fetch, and play time every single day, and has more energy than any dog I have ever seen. She's a total sweetheart, and loves to give lots of big wet kisses and cuddle close at night.

Our Princess Leia.

Randy and I found ourselves completely falling for her sweetness and loving personality. She loves us unconditionally, just as we love her. We're hooked, totally enamored with this sweet pooch. Randy especially enjoys having daily play and wrestle time with her. What a crazy pair they make.

During her stay with us, Leia became a sweet part of our daily lives and routine, and we quickly grew accustomed to her presence. When she went back to Chris and Myrna, our home suddenly seemed a bit strange and so quiet. It only took one month to really build that special relationship and bond. Leia's stay with us also turned out to be a valuable learning experience about what it takes to be a full-time owner of a young, larger-breed dog.

So, while I am not a current pet owner, I have a whole family of pets that are a special part of my life. We can love pets living within our home and those residing in the homes of those we love. Bringing home a new pet and adopting them into our lives is one of the most important decisions we will all face after we experience pet loss.

We must each decide what is right for us and when. Everyone is different.

FINANCES

When you bring a new pet into the home, there are added expenses. Think about vet visits, food, grooming, bedding, and toys. Will you be prepared to handle any medical needs that might arise? Have your finances changed recently?

LIFESTYLE

Think also about your current lifestyle. Are you busy and away from the home a significant amount of time? Do you travel often for business or pleasure? These are important questions, because the answers will affect how much time and energy you have to devote to a new pet companion. If you pick a pet with a high energy level, are you prepared for that activity requirement long term? That can also affect and directly impact the quality of your relationship.

FAMILY

Your family situation also determines whether you are ready for a new pet. Do you have a new baby on the way? Are your children getting ready to move out of the house? Who will be around for this new pet to interact and play with on a regular basis? These are all considerations to think about.

TRAVEL

If you travel regularly and can't bring the animal with you, you must think about who will care for it in your absence. If you use a boarding kennel, consider the cost. If you rely on a friend or family, think about how often you will need to do so. Are you being fair to the animal? Are you home enough to give it the proper care it needs? Will you be primarily an absentee pet owner?

HEALTH

Consider your health and how much it's changed since you last had a pet in your home. If you're facing significant health issues, is it a good idea to bring a new animal into your home? Can you properly care for it? You should also consider whether you'll be able to handle such a long-term commitment in the days to come.

Allergies

Having allergies to a specific breed doesn't always mean you can't have that kind of animal. You have to be proactive. It may mean that you have to clean a little more, have the animal groomed more frequently, invest in an air-filter purification system, or even get regular allergy shots. But if your allergies are more severe, debilitating, or contribute to a long-term health concern, you have to decide if it is worth having an animal in the home, or be willing to consider a breed of animal more conducive to your needs. There are various breeds that may be better suited to your medical needs.

ADOPTING FROM A SHELTER

When you are making the decision about bringing a new pet into the home, consider the option to adopt from a shelter or rescue. It is a wonderful thing to do, but you also must take a few things into consideration when going this route.

Whether you adopt or purchase your new friend, you cannot always assume the pet is healthy. Shelters will sometimes spay and neuter dogs, and while many also do certain tests to determine whether an animal is healthy, your new pet should immediately have a full and complete veterinary exam. Take your new pet to the vet as soon as possible after welcoming them into your home. Make no assumptions on your new pet's health status. Getting them checked out is a top priority. Get that communication going again with your vet to better understand their current health status and any particular needs they might have. Your vet will make sure your new friend is free of parasites or potentially harmful communicable diseases, to which children are particularly susceptible. Doing this immediately helps you catch any concerns early on and initiates that all-so-important vet/ pet relationship.

SERVICE, GUIDE, EMOTIONAL SUPPORT, AND ASSISTANCE ANIMALS

Service animals and guide dogs greatly increase the quality of life for their owners, but they offer much more than help with physical functions. The animal and the owner become extremely attached. The pain of losing the animal is magnified, because the pet owner has lost both a companion and someone who helps them navigate the world around them.

Pet owners want their new support animals quickly, because of the necessary service they provide, but unfortunately the process is not necessarily expedited quickly. Sometimes, matching the pet and owner can be a lengthy process. But even in these cases, the new bond cannot be rushed. People tend to assume the pairing of a service animal with their new owner is automatically a perfect match, but there's often an adjustment period for the owner and the new animal. He or she might still be grieving. This can be a significant emotional journey. For more information on service animals, please refer back to chapter 2.

Conclusion

If you can dream it, you can do it.
—WALT DISNEY

Years ago, when I was living in Venezuela, I tore the meniscus in both my knees. As a result, I needed to have surgery performed back home in the States, and I did not want to schedule two separate procedures. Two separate surgeries translated into two separate flights and two separate recovery journeys. I wanted it all over in one. I asked my doctor if I could please have them both done at the same time.

He was very hesitant, explaining he only performed surgery on one knee at a time for his patients. He had only done surgery on both knees once for one other patient, a cheerleader who had the full summer vacation off to recuperate and heal. With my prodding and unique circumstances, he eventually agreed. But he explained my recovery would be very difficult, because both knees needed to mend, and my initial mobility would be extremely limited. I would have to start riding a stationary bike the day after surgery to begin my recovery, and it was going to be tough. I told him I knew I could do it.

The surgery went well, and, as promised, I sat on the bike the next day at our hotel exercise facility prior to our return flight home. It soon became clear I had wildly underestimated just how hard riding it would be. The pain was so intense, it took me a full twenty minutes to complete one full rotation. I spent each of those twenty minutes with tears rolling down my face. But I could hear my doctor's voice saying, "You have to do this." So, I did.

The next day, riding the bike took me probably fifteen minutes. The next time, it took ten. Things were starting to slowly improve. I kept at it each day and never gave up. It was a process that involved horrible pain and extensive effort on my part, but it was necessary to heal. I was up to the challenge and determined to come out a winner.

Within a few weeks, I could do it with no pain at all, and today I can ride with no problems. In many ways, grief is like riding that bike. It's not fun, and it hurts initially, but if we diligently work at it, we can master it. We just must be resilient and remain willing to push forward, to overcome.

As I mentioned, Wookie was there, my sweet companion after my surgery—right there beside me, to comfort and ease my pain. She sensed I was struggling and knew I needed her. She was a friend in the truest sense. With memories like this, it is easy to understand why pet loss is so devastating and painful. Grief is not something to be avoided or ignored. The pain is not meant to be suppressed. It is a part of life, and we experience it for countless reasons.

Grief is normal. You must experience it to mend and recover. You must be willing to take responsibility for your own recovery by accepting your pet's loss or death and moving on. Nobody can fix you but you. You are responsible for your own life. Others will be monitoring your progress, including your children. By your diligent example, you provide them an opportunity to learn how to handle pain and grief as they watch you endure and positively press forward.

Once you do that, you can begin to ask questions that will start you on the healing process: "What am I going to do to get past this? I know it's going to be hard, so how do I take that first step?" Find sources for support and help. Talk to your spouse, your family, and your friends. Some of the best help you can get will be from those who knew your pet companion, had a connection with them, and appreciated them, as well as devoted friends who simply care, whether they knew your pet or not.

Remember that the loss of a pet is not always socially acknowledged or taken seriously. Not everyone will understand the level of grief you're experiencing. Remind yourself many people have never had the deep connection to a pet companion you have. Your bond was a gift; you were lucky to have it.

When you really start to take ownership of your grief and push yourself to take positive steps, you'll begin to see the positive results. You'll begin to notice yourself recovering. These changes won't be big or sudden. There will also be times when you feel like you're making progress, then something simple will throw you back into the heavy emotions of grief and loss. You need to surround yourself with love and those who can be there to support you. You need to let yourself cry, to let it all out so healing can begin.

Use your vet as a resource. They work with people going through similar situations on a regular basis, and they understand the pain you're feeling. Talk to them about what you're going through. If need be, they can recommend professional help as you work toward recovery.

There is no way to underestimate the value of a strong relationship with your vet. You have so much to learn from them, and those relationships will benefit us and our pets, especially, and most importantly when times are toughest.

As you complete the grieving cycle, you will reach a point where you can embrace the memories of the pet you lost and feel ready to move forward in new directions. This will be a strong indicator you're in a good place. When you reach it, your heart is healing, and perhaps ready to love again by welcoming another pet into your home.

If you decide to welcome a new companion into your home and your life, you will know when that time is right. But remember: life changes, things evolve, and so do people. There are times and seasons for all things. Whether we are young or old, there may be reasons why you do not get a new pet either now or in the future. It is a personal decision only you can make. The specific type of pet you adopt and bring into your home is another important decision. Consider this well and do the necessary research to make the best possible decision.

Getting to this stage happens at different times for different people. In certain circumstances, it is not necessarily the best decision to bring a new pet into their home. Not adopting a new pet into your life does not mean you do not love animals. It is a decision specific to your personal and unique needs. There should be no guilt, no matter what you decide. Be honest with yourself, and own your decision.

This book would never have come to be if we hadn't lost Wookie and taken the journey through the grief process. The journey has helped me appreciate Wookie, the unconditional love she showed, the companionship we shared, and the joy she brought me and countless others. I feel her presence every day. Even though she's not with us, I can still feel the joy she brought to our family.

I believe life is a journey. I liken it to the words of Thomas S. Monson:

Find joy in the journey.

I truly believe Wookie would be happy if this book helped you in any way. I hope it helps you to positively and actively engage in your recovery and healing process. I hope it helps you find peace and brings you closer to mending and piecing back together the parts of your broken heart.

Remember your own experiences, what you have learned in the process, and help others who have suffered the loss of a pet or other loved one. You've been through it, so you know what they need. When you provide that, you will feel as good as whomever you have served. Find your own personal "joy in the journey" by serving others. If this book has helped you, please recommend it to others who can benefit from it as well.

Always remember that you are capable of more than you know. You will get past this. You will overcome grief. The love you felt for your pet is a treasure, a gift beyond measure and it is the best tool you have against your pain.

Love lingers longer. Memories are meant to be cherished and broken hearts mend.

Acknowledgements

To everyone who helped, supported, and assisted me to make the publication of *Missing Pieces...Broken Heart* a reality. It is with sincere gratitude and deep appreciation I thank each and every one of you who have helped me along this journey.

Kathleen, my publisher, project manager, confidant, and friend, who kept this book on track and positively progressing forward. And put her heart into her work. You are amazing. We made the journey together.

Rachel, my insightful, diligent, and talented editor, who shared my vision and creativity. For being a good listener and friend. And for loving "great words and writing" as much as I do.

Tom, my talented outline editor, who helped me to meticulously organize my ideas and thoughts, and shared my vision as well.

Kevin, for his creative graphic touch and ability to bring my *kintsugi* heart to life in designing an amazing book cover.

Tucker, for believing in this book project from its conception and sharing his insight. And for always being there when questions came to mind. Your encouragement made a difference.

Tere, my incredibly talented "graphic guru," artist extraordinaire, and sweet friend. Magic happened with every photo you touched. You made my graphic dreams come to life.

They say it takes a village to raise a child.

And I believe it also it takes friends and family to be there to support and share your vision, and to help bring dreams to reality. I have been blessed with many.

Thanks to all those who shared their stories, experiences, and feelings; contributed a poem; wrote a letter or card; offered suggestions or ideas; listened when I needed a friend; showed compassion through their time, talents and gifts; and shared a piece of their hearts.

And to all my friends and family—children, grandchildren, and husband who knew and loved Wookie and have always been there for me:

Aaron, Ali, Andrew, Barbara, Brittany, Brooke, Cash, Charis, Chris, Christy, Dale, Doug, Emily, Emma, Eternity, Hannah, John, Kathleen, Kelli, LaMilla, Landon, Leila, Lisa, Logan, Maureen, Melanie, Melinda, Miller, Myrna, Patty, Phillip, Randy, Rose, Sarah, Stephanie, Taylor, Tristan, Tucker, Will.

And I would like to extend an extra measure of gratitude and a special thank you to those remarkable individuals who reached beyond the mark to support this book and partner with me to make it become a reality through contributing their wisdom, knowledge, medical expertise, and professional support.

Dr. Jessica Quillivan, DVM, who selflessly contributed extensive time proofreading the manuscript, for sharing your wisdom on pet loss and euthanasia, and offering insight on many of the special related needs of your clients, patients, veterinary staff, and animal caregivers alike. Your foreword is beautifully written with a professional polish, teamed with wisdom and important medical knowledge to support and educate pet owners. Your advice, compassionate care, and friendship were greatly appreciated when we lost Wookie under emergency circumstances.

Dr. Jose Salazar, DVM, who generously shared his time and offered insights and ideas on a wide variety of pet loss-related topics, such as: compassion fatigue, quality of life, end of life, and much more. Your input and suggestions were very important and relevant to the quality of the book. Your kindness and willingness to meet, discuss, and share information never wavered. As Wookie's final primary care veterinarian, you were a kindhearted friend and doctor, especially related to her quality of life decisions.

Dr. Sandy Block, DVM, your thoughts, input, ideas and suggestions, and professional advice and recommendations were impeccable. I will always be grateful for your medical skills and expertise in successfully removing Wookie's tumor when she had throat cancer. You took an extra measure of time and care talking about her surgery and aftercare. And you taught me much about euthanasia and anticipatory grief prior to euthanasia and the associated grief following this procedure.

Dr. Kim Eaton, DVM, your wisdom and knowledge shared were extensive. As we discussed quality of life, end of life, compassion fatigue, and adopting animals from shelters and rescue facilities, my eyes were opened. I learned so much from you and incorporated many ideas you graciously shared. Caring and your willingness to share important knowledge of the many aspects of animal care and pet loss made a difference. I will always remember you and your words about euthanasia, "it is the last gift of love…"

Tyler Patton, Publisher, Group Manager, your kindness, friendship, encouragement, and mentorship as my supervisor during my days as the Newspapers In Education manager and journalist for the *Odessa American* will always be remembered and greatly appreciated, along with your support for the book.

About the Author

B.J. SHONK has spent her professional career helping and mentoring others. As manager of the children's Newspaper In Education program and as a journalist for a Texas newspaper, she promoted literacy. Through her own business, she developed and implemented self-improvement and fitness-awareness programs for people of all ages. She is the mother of eight and grandmother of twelve—with four grand puppies and a grand kitty. Today, she lives in the Houston area with Randy, her husband of more than forty-five years. Together, they founded B J Randolph LLC for the purpose of sharing vision through knowledge and helping others.